TOP **10**
SEOUL

MARTIN ZATKO

EYEWITNESS TRAVEL

Left **Owl Art & Craft Museum** Center **Changdeokgung palace** Right **Jaunbong peak**

LONDON, NEW YORK,
MELBOURNE, MUNICH AND DELHI
www.dk.com

Printed and bound in China by
South China Printing Co. Ltd.

First American Edition, 2013
13 14 15 16 10 9 8 7 6 5 4 3 2 1

**Copyright 2013 © Dorling
Kindersley Limited, London
A Penguin Company**

Published in Great Britain
by Dorling Kindersley Limited

ISSN 1479-344X
ISBN 978 0 7566 9853 9

A catalog record for this book is available
from the Library of Congress.

Within each Top 10 list in this book, no
hierarchy of quality or popularity is implied.
All 10 are, in the editor's opinion, of roughly
equal merit.

Contents

Seoul's Top 10

The information in this DK Eyewitness Top 10 Travel Guide is checked regularly
Every effort has been made to ensure that this book is as up-to-date as possible at the time of
going to press. Some details, however, such as telephone numbers, opening hours, prices,
gallery hanging arrangements and travel information are liable to change. The publishers
cannot accept responsibility for any consequences arising from the use of this book, nor for
any material on third party websites, and cannot guarantee that any website address in this
book will be a suitable source of travel information. We value the views and suggestions of
our readers very highly. Please write to: Publisher, DK Eyewitness Travel Guides,
Dorling Kindersley, 80 Strand, London WC2R 0RL, or email: travelguides@dk.com

Cover: Front: **Corbis:** Topic Photo Agency (main), bl. Back: **Dorling Kindersley:** James Tye tc, tl, tr. Spine:
Dorling Kindersley: James Tye b.

Left **Seoul Land** Center **Ewha Womans University** Right **Korean dance performance**

Around Town

Streetsmart

Left **Noryangjin Fisheries Wholesale Market** Right **Throne Hall, Gyeongbokgung palace**

Key to abbreviations
Adm *admission charge*

3

SEOUL'S TOP10

TOP 10 Seoul's Highlights

Although justly regarded as one of the world's most modern cities, Seoul has a wealth of historic sights. Its two oldest and most splendid palaces – Gyeongbokgung and Changdeokgung – date back to the turn of the 15th century, as does Dongdaemun, Seoul's oldest existing city gate. The neighborhoods of Insadong, Bukchon, and Buamdong offer tantalizing hints of dynastic-era Korean life, while heading to the nearby city of Gwacheon will give you a break from the frenetic pace of the city.

Hangjidong

8 Buamdong

Cheongundong

Hongjedong

Inwangsan

Gyeongbokgung

Ever since its completion in 1394, the "Palace of Shining Happiness" has been a focal point of the city. Its halls and pavilions are superb examples of Buddhist decoration, and the museums are among the best in the land *(see pp8–9)*.

Insadong

Seoul's most popular tourist neighborhood is also one of its most traditional, with its zig-zagging lanes crammed with rustic restaurants, superb galleries, and handicraft stores *(see pp10–13)*.

National Museum of Korea

Korea's rich, colorful history is best explored in this gigantic museum, a repository of treasures from the various dynasties that have held power on the peninsula over the last 2,000 years *(see pp14–15)*.

Dongdaemun

Named after the ancient "Great East Gate" that still stands at its center today, this district is now more famous for its huge open-air market – offering everything from Korean food to silk *(see pp16–17)*.

Namsan

Rising from Seoul's very center and topped by the distinctive N Seoul Tower, this 860-ft (262-m-high) mountain *(above)* is the ideal place from which to survey the city, and its pine-lined trails are great for a gentle hike *(see pp18–19)*.

Preceding pages **Cherry blossoms in the Deoksugung palace complex**

Changdeokgung and Changgyeonggung
These UNESCO World Heritage-listed palaces are exactly what many visitors to Asia are looking for: great wooden architecture, perfectly manicured gardens, and the timeless air of dynasties long past *(see pp20–21)*.

Bukhansan National Park
Bukhansan is the world's most-visited national park. Temples, hermitages and Confucian academies stud its myriad hiking trails, which wind up toward a series of granite peaks *(see pp22–3)*.

Buamdong
Though just a hop, skip, and jump from Central Seoul, this neighborhood exudes the air of a provincial town. Its galleries, restaurants, cafés, and stores can easily take half a day to explore *(see pp24–5)*.

Bukchon Hanok Village
Korea's traditional wooden houses – *hanok* – are rare nowadays, but the narrow, hilly lanes of this charming area are lined with many pristine examples *(see pp26–9)*.

Gwacheon
Just south of Seoul is the leafy city of Gwacheon, home to an assortment of day-trip possibilities. Choose from a theme park, Seoul's only real zoo, one of the city's best contemporary art museums, a Confucian shrine, and the capital's largest tract of parkland *(see pp30–31)*.

TOP 10 Gyeongbokgung 경복궁

Taejo, the first king of the Joseon Dynasty, selected Seoul as his inaugural capital in 1392, and the construction of Gyeongbokgung – the "Palace of Shining Happiness" – was completed just two years later. This majestic structure has been of prime importance ever since, and served as the royal residence till 1910. The myriad wooden halls and gates dotting the complex are a riot of color, though in true Confucian style any opulence is balanced by nature – in this case, the pine-covered mountains which rise to its north.

Painted roof beams, Gyeongbokgung

🎧 Free English-language tours are offered outside the Gwanghwamun ticket booth at 11am, 1:30pm, and 3:30pm every day.

🍴 There is a quality restaurant within the National Palace Museum of Korea, and a small café inside the National Folk Museum. There are gift shops in both museums.

- Sajikro 161
- Map L1
- 732 1931
- Open Mar–May, Sep–Nov: 9am–5pm Mon–Sun; Jun–Aug: 9am–5:30pm Mon–Sun; Dec–Feb: 9am–4:30pm Mon–Sun • Adm: W3,000 (adults), W1,500 (7–19 year-olds); The palace is also accessible with the Integrated Palace Ticket (see p108)
- www.royalpalace.go.kr

Top 10 Features

1. Gwanghwamun
2. Gyeonghoeru
3. The Front Courtyard
4. Stonework
5. Geunjeongjeon Hall
6. The Northern Sector
7. Gangnyeongjeon Hall
8. Parujeong
9. National Folk Museum
10. National Palace Museum of Korea

1 Gwanghwamun

This imposing southern gate is one of Seoul's main landmarks. Destroyed and rebuilt several times through the ages, the current gate was unveiled in 2010, after four years of reconstruction.

2 Gyeonghoeru

This pavilion *(above)* was constructed in 1412, during the reign of King Taejong (1400–18), who hosted banquets and State meetings here. Located in the middle of a man-made lake, it is accessed via a stone bridge with ornately carved balustrades.

3 The Front Courtyard

During the day, visitors buy tickets for the palace here. In the evening, it is perhaps Seoul's best spot for viewing the sunset – the grand palace fading against the setting sun makes for a striking sight.

4 Stonework

An assortment of sculptures *(below)* – both traditional and contemporary in design – can be found just north of the National Palace Museum of Korea. This is a grassy area, ideal for picnicking.

5 Geunjeongjeon Hall

This huge two-tiered structure was the former throne room *(left)* of the palace. Inside, a beautiful folding screen is placed behind the Joseon throne, featuring the sun, the moon, and five mountains painted onto a dark blue background.

6 The Northern Sector

In this little-visited sector of the complex, many buildings which were destroyed in the Japanese occupation of Korea have been reconstructed. They exude a timeless air and are worth a visit.

7 Gangnyeongjeon Hall

Constructed in 1395, Gangnyeongjeon Hall was used as a bed chamber by several Joseon kings. It was rebuilt in 1995 and redecorated with original dynastic furnishings.

8 Parujeong

One of the most distinctive buildings in the complex, this two-storied octagonal structure *(right)* was built in 1888 and used as a library by King Gojong. Interestingly, its design is more suggestive of the Chinese Qing dynasty than Joseon-era Korea.

A Turbulent History

Given what it has been through, it is something of a miracle that Gyeongbokgung still stands. The first major issue was the disastrous fire of 1553, followed by the Japanese invasion of the 1590s which saw much of the palace razed to the ground. All but 10 buildings were destroyed during the Japanese occupation of Korea (1910–45), which was followed by the devastating Korean War. Major reconstruction has been underway since 1989, and half of the palace's buildings are already back in place.

9 National Folk Museum

This museum has an assortment of original dynastic clothing, as well as hands-on displays that are popular with kids *(left)*.

10 National Palace Museum of Korea

Over 40,000 artifacts from Seoul's five palaces, spanning the 500-year reign of the Joseon dynasty, are housed here. Look out for statues, scrolls, and fragments of the original palace woodwork.

TOP 10 **Insadong** 인사동

Seoul's most popular tourist district, and with good reason, Insadong is by far the most interesting and quintessentially Korean place in the city to shop or eat. Most of this area is made up of narrow, winding alleys known as golmok, which are a delight to wander about in. These lanes are filled to the brim with small charming galleries, restaurants, tearooms, and trinket shops, and some are even housed in traditional wooden hanok buildings.

Butterfly trinkets in a shop in Insadong

🕐 **Insadong is least crowded just before sunset.**

- Map M3 • Insa Art Center: 29–23 Gwanhundong; 735 2655; Open 10am–6:30pm Mon–Sat, 10:30am–6pm Sun; Adm
- Jogyesa: Gyeonjidong 45; 732 2183
- Yetchatjip: 2F 196–5 Gwanhundong; 722 5332; Open 10am–11pm daily • Balwoo Gongyang: 71 Gyeonjidong; 2031 2081
- Unhyeongung: 114–10 Unnidong; 766 9090; Open Nov–Mar: 9am–5:30pm Tue–Sun, Apr–Oct: 9am–6:30pm Tue–Sun; Adm
- Min's Club: Gyeongundong; 733 2966; Open noon–10:30pm daily (orders noon–2:30pm & 6–9:30pm only)
- Story of the Blue Star: 734 3095; Open noon–3pm, 6pm–10pm daily
- Ssamziegil: Gwanhundong 38; 736 0088; Open 10am–8:30pm daily

Top 10 Features

Insa Art Center
1 The largest gallery in Insadong, this is also the most interesting – exhibitions change weekly *(above)*.

Tapgol Park
2 Named after a 15th-century relic – a stone pagoda from the Buddhist temple once located here – this park *(above)* hosted a protest against Japanese occupation in 1919.

Jogyesa
3 Seoul's most prominent temple *(main image)* is the head-quarters of the Jogye order, Korea's primary Buddhist sect. The main hall is a fantastic example of the country's colorful and immaculately painted temple decorations.

Yetchatjip
4 This tearoom's claim to fame are the dozen or so small birds that fly around it freely. The herbal infusions it offers are also excellent.

5 Balwoo Gongyang

The best of Seoul's vegetarian "temple food" restaurants, Balwoo Gongyang *(left)* peers out over Jogyesa – the ideal setting. The food is good and dishes are served in the wooden bowls from which the restaurant takes its name.

6 Unhyeongung

Seoul's unofficial sixth palace, Unhyeongung *(above)* was denied the title as it was never occupied by a king. Though not as striking as the others, it is charming and has a tranquil atmosphere, making it worth a visit.

7 Min's Club

This splendid restaurant *(below)* is housed in a 1920s *hanok*, which, though ancient-looking now, was quite innovative at that time. The luxurious interior makes a superb backdrop while sampling wines from the lengthy list.

8 Story of the Blue Star

A local favorite, this tiny restaurant serves mountain food and interesting *makgeolli* infusions. The menu is written in Korean, in a calligraphic style, on the walls.

Avoid-Horse Alley

Jongno, in the heart of Insadong, has been Seoul's most important road since ancient times. Aristocrats, known as *yangban*, would glide along the road on their horses, and as they passed, commoners were required to prostrate themselves before them. Eventually, thoroughfares hidden from *yangban* view were created. Pimatgol, a side-street just north of Jongno, and running parallel to it, literally translates to "avoid-horse alley."

9 Ssamziegil

Popular with Korean youth and tourists, this handicrafts market *(below)* is essentially a single path that spirals up through four floors. In addition to shops, the complex has a few good restaurants on the upper level.

10 Sunday Visits

Traffic is barred from entering Insadonggil on Sundays, making it a good day to visit. In warmer months, you might even see a parade or a musical display here.

Left **Calligraphic paper** Center **Sun Gallery and Art Center** Right **Art supplies at a shop**

🔟 Insadong Souvenirs

1 Art Supplies
Insadong's area has long been a favorite with local artists, and has dozens of art-supplies shops that cater to their needs. Apart from high-quality paints and paper, these shops also sell a range of excellent brushes.

2 Name Chops
Some art-supplies shops also sell name chops. Made from marble, jade, and other stones, these are still used across East Asia today in lieu of a signature. If requested, these can be inscribed with foreign names, in either Roman or Korean characters.

Name chops

3 Tea Sets
There is a tremendous range of tea sets in Insadong, and they are among the most popular purchases by visitors. Head to Insadonggil for the inexpensive ones, or to shops such as Yido Pottery *(see p72)*, Kwang Ju Yo, and the Korea Culture & Design Foundation *(see p72)* for designer fare.

Hanbok, Korea's national dress

4 Traditional clothing
The strikingly colorful *hanbok* is the national dress of Korea. Insadong has several tailors who can make this outfit, although commissioning one may be a little expensive. It's a better idea to check out one of the stores in the area selling contemporary styles; try Sami *(see p72)* for wearable options.

5 Pendants and Jewelry
Insadong is a great place for jewelry – a stroll around the bustling Ssamziegil complex *(see p11)* will reveal a variety of shops selling styles from traditional to contemporary. Visitors should also look out for stores selling tiny silk pendants – these make attractive and inexpensive souvenirs.

Buddhist Regalia

The most important Buddhist temple in the city, Jogyesa *(see p10)* lies on the western fringe of the Insadong area. There is a clutch of shops near the temple, selling traditional Buddhist paraphernalia. Although these are intended for the benefit of worshippers, the clothing, incense, and bronzeware is sure to interest visitors as well.

Buddhist statuettes

Handmade Paper

Koreans are proud of their local paper; known as *hanji*, it is usually made from mulberry leaves. You can buy entire rolls of this from the art-supplies shops, but non-artists will doubtless be more interested in items made with *hanji* – including lanterns, hand fans, calligraphic scrolls, and figurines.

Rice Cakes

Rice cakes play an important role in the life of Koreans – they form part of many meals, and are used as table decorations during holidays and coming-of-age ceremonies. Bizeun *(see p72)* sells ready-to-eat rice cakes as well as takeaway souvenir packs, and the many rustic stores around Fraser Suites *(see p114)* sell cheaper versions of the same.

Paintings

Insadong is packed with art galleries, and a few places offer visitors the chance to purchase local art. While the basement of the Ssamziegil complex *(see p11)* is a good place to go looking, most of the area's smaller, more independent galleries are also worth a visit.

Pottery

Korean pottery has been admired since the time of the Three Kingdoms, and is popular to this day. A couple of shops, located just north of the main Insadong area, are superb places for pottery shopping – Yido Pottery *(see p72)* has a fantastic range of earthenware. Also definitely worth visiting, the smaller, classier Kwang Ju Yo shop is down the road *(see p72)*.

Ceramic ware on display, Yido Pottery

TOP10 **National Museum of Korea**
국립중앙박물관

Korea's National Museum is, by far, the country's most important repository of historical artifacts. Once housed in the grounds of Gyeongbokgung Palace, it moved in 2005 to a state-of-the-art facility on land previously owned by the American Army. A trove of treasures, it gives visitors a chronological tour through Korean history – from the Paleolithic to the Three Kingdoms period, and then through the Silla, Goryeo, and Joseon dynasties.

View of the museum and pagoda from the lake

🧭 Pick up pamphlets and leaflets from the information desk in the main lobby.

🍴 The museum has several options for refreshment – there's a trendy café up the stairs from the main entrance, a tearoom at the opposite end of the first floor, a good restaurant overlooking the lake outside the museum, and a convenience store for snacks.

• 168–6 Yongsandong
• Map C4
• 2077 9000
• Open 9am–6pm Tue, Thu & Fri, 9am–9pm Wed & Sat, 9am–7pm Sun • English-language hourly tours of the museum start at 10:30am and 2:30pm
• www.museum.go.kr

Top 10 Features
1. Comb-Pattern Pottery
2. Silla Jewelry
3. Baekje Ornaments
4. Ten-Level Pagoda
5. Metal Type
6. Pensive Bodhisattva
7. Joseon's Basic Code of Laws
8. Kim Hong-do's Genre Paintings
9. Buddhist Paintings
10. Dynastic Pottery

1 Comb-Pattern Pottery
Dating back to 5,000 BC, these earthenware jars, decorated with a zigzag pattern, were used to store and carry food. These are among the earliest Korean archaeological finds.

2 Silla Jewelry
The Silla dynasty unified the Korean peninsula c. 660. Their jewelry was similar to that of the Baekje dynasty, and is best exemplified by decorative crowns *(above)* and earrings.

3 Baekje Ornaments
Kings of the Baekje dynasty (18 BC – AD 660) had a penchant for golden accessories in an Art Nouveau style *(above)*. The headgear found inside the tomb of King Muryeong in Gongju *(see p63)* is a good example.

4 Ten-Level Pagoda
A gigantic Buddhist pagoda *(main image)*, first erected in 1348 during the Goreyo dynasty (918–1392), is the centerpiece of the museum.

5 Metal Type
A Buddhist document, *Jikji*, printed in 1377, was the world's first book printed with movable type *(below)*. The museum has pieces of the original metal type.

Key
- First Floor
- Second Floor
- Third Floor

6 Pensive Bodhisattva
Displayed in a room of its own on the third floor, this finely worked figurine *(right)* is made of bronze and was cast in the early 7th century. It is one of the most cherished items in the museum.

7 Joseon's Basic Code of Laws
During the Joseon dynasty Korean society became highly Confucian in nature. A series of documents showcases the rituals that were common in society at that time.

9 Buddhist Paintings
The Buddhist painting room on the second floor has a series of elaborate and colorful Buddhist scrolls and folding screens from the Goryeo and Joseon periods.

8 Kim Hong-do's Genre Paintings
Genre paintings by Kim Hong-do (1745–1806) are revered by museum curators. These simple illustrations *(above)* perfectly evoke the clothing, gestures, and practises of the time.

10 Dynastic Pottery
Dynastic-era pottery *(left)* fills several halls on the museum's third floor. Korean artisans worked with porcelain and celadon, but some of their techniques remain a mystery even today.

The Many Names of Seoul
Seoul has had many names. Known as Wiryeseong under the Baekje kings (18 BC–AD 660), its name changed to Hanju in Silla times (660–918) and to Namgyeong under the Goryeo dynasty (918–1392). It was known as Hanseong, then Hanyang, under Joseon rule (1392–1910), and as Keijo under Japanese occupation (1910–45).

Dongdaemun 동대문

An elaborately painted, two-tiered structure that once marked the eastern perimeter of Seoul, Dongdaemun literally means the "Great East Gate." The city may have expanded but the gate, dating from 1398, is still here despite being wrecked by fire, restored, and rebuilt again in 1869. Today it represents an interesting mix of renovation and reconstruction. The gigantic market area that has developed around Dongdaemun is one of the most fascinating places in all of Korea.

Diners in Woo Lae Oak

⊙ There are a number of excellent restaurants in the area, including Woo Lae Oak and Samarkand *(see p79).* For a simpler meal, head to Gwangjang Market.

• Map D2
• Dongdaemun Market: Shops: Open 8am–6pm daily; Food Court: Open 7am–7pm daily
• Gwangjang Market: Open 9am–6pm (opening hours may vary from store to store)
• Lantern Festival: Held mid-May each year (dates may vary)

Top 10 Features

1. Dongdaemun
2. Dongdaemun Market
3. Gwangjang Market
4. Dongdaemun Design Plaza
5. Dongdaemun Design Park
6. Russia Town
7. City Walls
8. Cheonggyecheon
9. Lantern Festival
10. Furniture District

Dongdaemun

This gigantic ornamental gate was known as Heunginjimun in the past *(right).* It now sits at the heart of the city district that goes by the same name.

Gwangjang Market

A shopping area, Gwangjang consists of two intersecting covered arcades, from which innumerable side-alleys and mini-alleys sprout. If you can bear the gritty atmosphere of the restaurants and stalls *(below),* they are fascinating places to eat in. The alleys are home to hundreds of fabric stores.

Dongdaemun Market

To the south of the gate, you can see a series of high-rise malls *(above).* They sell inexpensive copies of branded goods and are extremely popular with locals and visitors alike.

4 Dongdaemun Design Plaza

Located to the south of Dongdaemun gate, this structure, designed by architect Zaha Hadid, is an urban development project currently under construction. It is expected to be a major convention hall and design hub.

5 Dongdaemun Design Park

Previously a baseball stadium, this landscaped area surrounds the Design Plaza *(above)*, and is being developed into a cultural space.

6 Russia Town

The area west of Dongdaemun Design Plaza has been given this name due to the Cyrillic signs on display there *(below)*. However, most traders here are from Mongolia and Uzbekistan.

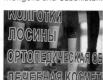

7 City Walls

Seoul's giant gates were once portals through a fortress-like wall that encircled the city. There's a remodeled section stretching north of Dongdaemun – follow the quiet roads west up to Naksan Park for lovely views of this stretch.

8 Cheonggyecheon

Starting just south of Gwanghwamun station, this stream *(below)* runs for 5 miles (8 km) below street level. The path alongside is a delight for pedestrians.

Seoul Under Curfew

Today, Dongdaemun is bang in the center of the city, and the market around it buzzes with activity all day and night. However, during the dynastic-era, Dongdaemun not only marked the far eastern edge of the city, but the area surrounding the gate was also shut at sundown at the tolling of a bell. This gave its name to Jongno (Bell Street), which lies west of the gate (see p11).

9 Lantern Festival

In recent years, Seoul has put on spectacular lantern festivals on Cheonggyecheon, featuring a mix of traditional designs and animal floats.

10 Furniture District

Step outside Euljiro 4-ga subway station's south-facing exits and enter the city's furniture district, where dozens of shops sell nothing but home furnishings.

10 **Namsan** 남산

Given that mountains make up most of Korea's landmass, it is hardly a surprise to find one right in the middle of Seoul. Namsan, a 860-ft (262-m) high peak, once marked the city's southern edge. Nowadays it is home to a variety of interesting sights: the iconic N Seoul Tower sprouts from Namsan's summit; its slopes are a veritable maze of delightful hiking trails; while on the foothills you will find a traditional performance hall and some enchanting wooden hanok buildings.

View of N Seoul Tower

🐦 Namsan's summit can be crowded around sunset; try coming for sunrise instead.

🍴 There are snack bars in and around N Seoul Tower and near the lower terminus of the cable car.

• 100–177 Hoehyeondong 1-ga
• Map D3 • 3455 9277
• N Seoul Tower: Open 10am–11pm Mon–Thu & Sun, 10am–midnight Fri & Sat • N Grill: 3455 9297; Open 11am–2pm & 5–11pm daily
• Teddy Bear Museum: Open 10am–10pm Mon–Thu & Sun, 10am–11pm Fri & Sat; Adm
• Namsangol Hanok Village: 2264 4412; Open Apr–Oct: 9am–9pm Wed–Mon, Nov–Mar: 9am–8pm Wed–Mon
• Namsan Cable Car: Open 10am–11pm daily; Adm; Ohreumi Elevator: 9am–11:30pm daily
• National Theater: 2280 4114

Top 10 Features

1. N Seoul Tower
2. Mongmyeoksan Beacon Towers
3. Walking Paths
4. Dongguk University
5. Namsangol Hanok Village
6. Namsan Gugakdang
7. Locks of Love
8. Namsan Cable Car
9. National Theater
10. Teddy Bear Museum

N Seoul Tower 1

Seoul's best-known landmark stands like a gigantic needle atop Namsan's summit *(main image)*. Its observation deck offers superb views and there are many dining and entertainment options inside, including the N Grill restaurant.

Mongmyeoksan Beacon Towers 2

These chimney-like stone towers *(above)* date back to the Joseon era. They were part of a larger, elaborate series of towers that were used to relay warnings across the peninsula, from one mountaintop to another.

Walking Paths 3

Namsan's slopes are covered with great walking paths, but it is possible to lose your way. While heading upwards will bring you to the top, heading down can be tricky.

Dongguk University 4

Located at the foot of Namsan, this is one of the most prestigious educational institutions in South Korea.

5 Namsangol Hanok Village

This cluster of wooden buildings *(left)* are genuine abodes from the Joseon dynasty that were relocated here from other parts of Seoul. You can see how Seoul used to look, and also take part in simple traditional games.

Chungmuro Ⓜ

TOEGYENO 5 6 Dongguk University Ⓜ

SOPAJO DONGGUL 4

8

1 2 9

7 10 3

SOWOLGIL *Namsan Park* ITAEWONGIL

HOENAMUGIL Hangangjin

6 Namsan Gugakdang

Located in the park area behind Namsangol, Namsan Gugakdang *(below)* is Seoul's most traditional performance hall – "*gugak*" means "national music" in Korean. Performances are diverse, but are always interesting to watch.

7 Locks of Love

The top of Namsan has countless "trees" covered with padlocks *(above)*, which symbolize eternal love. Couples buy a lock, write a message on it, and then attach the lock to one of the "trees" and throw away the keys. The spot is extremely popular with visitors and locals alike.

8 Namsan Cable Car

The cable car is a fun way to ascend Namsan. Though its lower terminus is a fair way above street level, it can be reached via the Ohreumi elevator – the entrance is a short walk from Myeongdong subway station.

9 National Theater

Located on Namsan's eastern flank, this is among Korea's foremost performance venues. It is also an entry point for the mountain's most popular walking path.

10 Teddy Bear Museum

Located in the N Seoul Tower, this is one of Seoul's more curious museums. As the name suggests, it is dedicated to teddy bears and there are all sorts on display *(left)*.

Smoke Signals

During the Joseon era, Koreans used smoke signals to communicate, and Namsan was the fulcrum of a nationwide network of chimneys used to signal warnings. Depending upon the perceived level of threat, between one and five beacons would be lit; the signal would then be copied at beacons on successive mountainsides, all the way up to the coasts and the Chinese border.

🔟 Changdeokgung & 창덕궁 Changgyeonggung 창경궁

Two of Seoul's five royal palaces, Changdeokgung and Changgyeonggung, are separated only by a wall. Though their names sound similar, there is plenty to distinguish between the two. Completed in 1412, Changdeokgung is the older of the pair, and the best-kept of Seoul's palaces. Changgyeonggung, on the other hand, completed in 1483, is a humbler palace and is connected by footbridge to Jongmyo, a park-like compound that serves as a shrine for the kings of Joseon.

Changdeokgung Palace

Changdeokgung can only be visited as part of a guided tour, except on Thursdays, but for five times the price. There are monthly night tours of Changdeokgung. Both the palaces and Jongmyo can be visited with the Integrated Palace Ticket (see p108).

• Changdeokgung: 110–360 Yulgokro 99; Map P2; 762 8261; Open Apr–Sep: 9am–5:30pm, Oct: 9am–5pm, Nov & Mar: 9am–5:30pm, Dec–Feb: 9am–4pm (closed Mon); Adm: W3,000, Secret Garden: W2,000; eng.cdg.go.kr
• Changgyeonggung: 2–1 Waryongdong; Map P2; 762 4868; Open Apr–Oct: 9am–5:30pm, Nov & Mar: 9am–5:30pm, Dec–Feb: 9am–5pm (closed Mon); Adm: W1,000, Jongmyo: W1,000.

Top 10 Features

1. Donhwamun
2. The Secret Garden
3. Injeongjeon
4. Geumcheongyo
5. Huijeongdang
6. Myeongjeongjeon
7. Munjeongjeon
8. Changgyeonggung Greenhouse
9. Jongmyo
10. Jongmyo Park

Donhwamun
Originally built in 1412, Changdeokgung's huge, two-tiered main gate was burned down during the 1592 Japanese invasions, rebuilt in 1607, and finally restored in 1609.

The Secret Garden
Created as a place of pleasure for kings, this garden (above) is centered on a stunning lotus pond and is Changdeokgung's pride and joy.

Injeongjeon
Although ravaged by fire several times, Changdeokgung's throne room (main image) remains truly spectacular. Inside, there is a replica of a folding screen that the Joseon kings used as a backdrop to their thrones.

Geumcheongyo
A 600-year-old granite bridge, this is one of the few survivors from Changdeokgung's original construction. The animal faces carved into various points of the bridge are typical of the early Joseon period.

Huijeongdang

5 This hall in Changdeokgung *(above)* was used by several kings of the late Joseon period and, somewhat incongruously, features Western-style carpets, floorboards, and chandeliers.

Myeongjeongjeon

6 Changgyeonggung has an older main hall than any other Seoul palace – it is also the smallest, since this single-level structure was supposed to be the living quarters of the dowager queen.

Munjeongjeon

7 In 1762, Prince Sado – heir to the throne – was killed at his father's behest at Munjeongjeon, a gate protruding from the Changgyeonggung palace walls.

Changgyeonggung Greenhouse

8 To the north of Changgyeonggung is a Victorian-style greenhouse. Built in 1907, it is now home to over one hundred species of plants.

Jongmyo

9 This Confucian shrine has two main halls that house the "spirit tablets" of all Joseon kings. Every ruling king came by five times a year to pay his respects to his predecessors. A re-creation of this ceremony, known as Jongmyo Daejae, now takes place each May *(see p36).*

Jongmyo Park

10 This small area *(below)* outside Jongmyo's entrance is frequented by elderly Korean men on sunny days.

Palace or Theme Park?

Changgyeonggung's greenhouse predates the Japanese occupation by three years, but it became a symbol of the oppression that followed. In an attempt to sully the dignity of Korea's royal line, the Japanese turned the palace into a theme park of sorts, with the greenhouse as a focal point. While it is viewed as an unacceptable slight against the nation today, the theme park was enjoyed until the early 1980s – almost 40 years after the end of occupation.

TOP 10 Bukhansan National Park
북한산 국립 공원

Seoul is a rarity among world capitals, in that it boasts a national park within the city limits. The park is split into distinct northern and southern sections, although both offer the same charms – a series of mountain trails, freshwater streams, rippling tendons of rock, granite peaks, and a clutch of functional Buddhist temples and hermitages. The trails are ideal – simple enough for hiking novices, yet steep enough to provide a good workout.

Shops selling hiking gear inside the park

🦋 In good weather, the park is crammed with visitors on weekends. Visit on a weekday if possible.

🍴 There are restaurants outside all major entrances, and drinking-water springs are found on many trails. All temples have coffee machines and Cheonchuksa even offers free cinnamon punch.

• Map G1
• Bukhansan National Park Office: San 1–1, Jeongneungdong; 909 0497
• Rock Climbing: www. koreaontherocks.com

Top 10 Features

1. Dobong Seowon
2. Northern Ridgeway
3. Jaunbong
4. Mangwolsa
5. Streams and Waterfalls
6. Cheonchuksa
7. Bukhansanseong Trail
8. Baekundae
9. Rock Climbing
10. Mountain Food

Dobong Seowon
Confucian academies, known as *seowon*, were once the backbone of the educational system but were restricted to the aristocrats. This relic *(above)*, near the Dobongsan park entrance, is a remnant of that time.

Northern Ridgeway
A ridge trail runs for 6 miles (9 km) from the Uidong entrance to Wongaksa temple – start early to complete it within the day. On the way there are three major peaks, many smaller crests, and a few Buddhist temples.

Jaunbong
At a height of 2,430 ft (740 m) above sea-level, Jaunbong *(below)* is the highest peak both along the ridgeway and in the park's northern section.

4 Mangwolsa

Located between the Northern Ridgeway and a subway station named after it, Mangwolsa temple is the park's focal point for hikers. On the way up, follow the Wondobong valley trail, which features a few freshwater springs.

5 Streams and Waterfalls

Valleys snake off the park's long ridge trails, and many feature streamside walking trails and, in some cases, small waterfalls. The streams are perfect to dip your feet in after a tough hike.

6 Cheonchuksa

Perhaps the most distinctive of Bukhansan's several temples, Cheonchuksa *(above)* is also one of the oldest, dating to 673 BC. It is located under Seoninbong, a granite peak.

8 Baekundae

At 2,746 ft (837 m), Baekundae *(above)* is the park's high point and part of the Bukhansanseong Trail. It is no surprise that the views from here are breathtaking.

9 Rock Climbing

Bukhansan's southern section, particularly the area around Insubong, is becoming popular with rock climbers, though the activity is still pretty new to South Korea. The Korea on The Rocks website has details.

7 Bukhansanseong Trail

In the early days of the Joseon dynasty a fortress wall was built in Bukhansan to protect Seoul from invaders. Renovated many times since, its contours form a delightful hiking trail.

Education in the Joseon Era

In the days of the dynasty, education was restricted to the children of yangban – the aristocratic elite – who studied in Confucian academies known as *seowon*. Tests were difficult to pass – even Yi Hwang (1501–70), one of Seoul's most revered scholars, took four years to pass his preliminary government exams, and another seven to become a civil servant.

10 Mountain Food

In Korea, it is a custom to eat *pajeon* (pancakes) after a hike. If you prefer mountain fare, many restaurants serve *sanchae bibimbap* *(above)*, a take on *bibimbap* (see p42).

TOP 10 **Buamdong** 부암동

During the early years of Korea's economic boom, Buamdong and the neighboring Pyeongchangdong district were considered Seoul's most luxurious places to live – one reason for the presence there of a series of larger-than-usual houses and ornate villas. Young Seoulites visit in droves on weekends, punctuating their strolls with visits to the area's quirky cafés and bars.

Exterior of Whanki Art Gallery

⊘ Come to Buamdong during the week if you can. It is a tremendously popular target for weekend jaunts, and crowds can dilute the area's appeal.

• Whanki Art Gallery: 210–8 Buamdong; Map C1; 391 7702; Open 10am–6pm Tue–Sun; www.whankimuseum.org
• Gana Art Gallery: 97 Pyeongchangdong; 720 1020; Open 10am–7pm Mon–Sun; www.ganaart.com
• Sanmotoonge: 97–5 Buamdong; Map C1; 391 4737; Open 11am–10pm daily

Top 10 Features

1. Whanki Art Gallery
2. Gana Art Gallery
3. Bugaksan
4. Jahamun Gate
5. Dining
6. Sanmotoonge
7. Baeksasil Valley Walk
8. Inwangsan
9. Typography
10. Pyeongchangdong Villas

Whanki Art Gallery
Kim Whanki was part of the Paris avant-garde movement in the 1930s, and brought Western ideas and techniques back to Korea. This superb gallery is devoted to his works.

Gana Art Gallery
South Korea's largest gallery is tucked into mountain foothills, and the fewer crowds help ensure there is space to appreciate the gallery's exhibits.

Bugaksan
Once Seoul's northern boundary, this mountain is home to restored portions of the fortress walls *(main image)*. Security is high here so carry your ID.

Jahamun Gate
This large gate *(above)* once marked the northern end of Seoul. Its splendid paint and stonework stand out within its natural setting.

Dining

5 Buamdong has become very trendy in recent years, and is popular with couples on a date. You will find Italian food on most menus, but Jaha Sonmandoo's *(see p71)* dumplings, usually served in casseroles *(left)*, are more appropriate to the scenery.

Sanmotoonge

6 In a city filled with high-rises, it's astonishingly hard to find a café with a view. Head to Sanmotoonge, where outdoor tables afford amazing vistas of the Bukhansan mountain range to the north *(above)*.

Baeksasil Valley Walk

7 This mostly flat trail takes around two hours, and on the way you'll pass by streams, picnic places, and a couple of temples.

From Pyongyang With Love

An idyllic place today, Bugaksan mountain holds a nasty secret. In 1968, it was the scene of an assassination attempt on the life of then-president Park Chung-hee. A team of North Korean commandos had crossed the border and made their way down to Seoul; by the time they were apprehended, they were just 2,624 ft (800 m) from the presidential abode. Almost 100 were killed as the team tried, in vain, to head back to the DMZ *(see p62)*.

Inwangsan

8 The Buamdong area is also a starting point for the trails of Inwangsan, one of Seoul's most important religious mountains *(above)*.

Typography

9 The neon signs seen nearly everywhere in Seoul are absent here. Typography comes in the old painted and metal forms – look out for the simple whitewash-on-brick logo of Hanyang Ricecake Shop.

Pyeongchangdong Villas

0 Buamdong's neighboring district, Pyeongchangdong sports a few large *hanok* villas that were built in the old days before the advent of high-rise apartments *(above)*.

和10 Bukchon Hanok Village
북촌 한옥 마을

Bukchon is an island of tradition in modern Seoul. Hanok, the wooden houses that once blanketed Korea, have now largely been replaced with concrete towers, making Bukchon a living museum of historic Korean architecture. You'll see hanok aplenty here; while most are functioning homes, some have been converted into charming cafés, tearooms, and galleries.

Hanok door with lantern decorations

🍵 There are plenty of *hanok* cafés and tearooms in Bukchon Hanok Village – try **Books Cooks** *(see p53)* for English tea and scones, **LN** *(see p73)* for coffee, or **Cha Masineun Tteul** *(see p50)* for traditional Korean tea.

ℹ️ Several information booths dot the area. The ones uphill from Anguk station's exit 2 and the Arario Gallery are the most accessible.

• All sights here are within walking distance of Anguk subway station (line 3, exits 1 and 2).
• Map M1

Top 10 Features

1. Views
2. Night Visits
3. Pottery
4. Choong-Ang High School
5. Changdeokgung Views
6. Samcheongdong
7. Samcheong Park
8. Hanjeongsik
9. Tearooms
10. Galleries and Museums

Views 1
The maze-like alleys of the Bukchon neighborhood *(main image)* are a delight to wander. Though there are eight officially designated "Viewing Spots," stroll around and you will doubtless come across your own splendid vista.

2 Night Visits
The Bukchon area is hugely popular with locals, and during the daytime it can become a little crowded. Visit at night, when the area is almost deserted, and the *hanok* houses look even more spectacular.

3 Pottery
The Bukchon area offers some wonderful shopping opportunities, particularly if you are looking for some high-quality pottery – Kwang Ju Yo *(right)* and Yido are the pick of the bunch *(see p72).*

4 Choong-Ang High School
At the top of the Bukchon area is this prestigious school, with its Gothic-style main hall. Built in 1937, it is one of Seoul's most beautiful Colonial-era buildings designed in a western architectural style. A functioning school, it can only be visited on weekends.

➡️ *Houses are known as "ok" in Korean, and the prefix, "han," meaning "Korean," was added later to describe traditional abode.*

Changdeokgung Views

5 Head to the sports field behind Choong-Ang High School and you'll be afforded a unique, and rather breathtaking, view of the off-limits northwestern corner of Changdeokgung palace *(left)*. The largest hall you can see is the Sinseonwonjeon, which was used to house official portraits of the kings of Joseon *(see pp20–21)*.

Samcheongdong

6 Adjoining Bukchon is Samcheongdong *(above)*, run-down for decades but now bursting with funky cafés and restaurants. It's a great place for a stroll.

Samcheong Park

7 Samcheongdonggil – the main road in the Samcheongdong area – goes up to Samcheong Park, a pleasant space. Paths lead from here to Seoul's old city wall.

Hanjeongsik

8 In the alleys near Anguk subway station are several *hanok*-style restaurants serving *hanjeongsik* – traditional Korean meals.

Galleries and Museums

10 As well as large galleries, the area also has small, private art spaces and museums *(see pp28–9)*, most with wonderfully quirky artifacts *(above)*.

Tearooms

9 Insadong, to the south, may have a wider variety of tearooms, but experiencing a traditional tea in Seoul's most traditional area is a delight *(above)*. Meander through Bukchon's winding alleyways, and stop at one for a break.

Hanok Housing

Most *hanok* have a central, dirt courtyard. Rooms are arrayed around it, each with sloping roofs of stacked slate on plaster and wooden beams. Between vertical beams of wood are walls of mud and plaster, covered on the inside with sheaves of mulberry paper. More such paper lines the floor, varnished to a yellow glaze and heated from beneath by wood fires.

Left **Display at World Jewellery Museum** Center **Exterior, Kukje Gallery** Right **Arario Gallery**

Bukchon's Galleries and Museums

Gallery Hyundai
갤러리 현대

The oldest commercial gallery in the country, Hyundai is one of South Korea's best show-cases of local art. Its large halls display a variety of exhibitions, though paintings from the latter third of the 20th century – usually distinctly Korean in appearance – are what the gallery is known for. It has two other annexes showing more contemporary fare.

◈ *122 Sagandong • Map L2 • 734 6111*
• Open 10am–6pm Tue–Sun
• Adm • www.galleryhyundai.com

Gahoe Museum 가회박물관
Housed in a *hanok*, this museum is filled with over 1,500 works of local art, including folk paintings, folding screens, and a collection of traditional amulets.
◈ *11–103 Gahoedong • Map M1 • 741 0466 • Open 10am–6pm Tue–Sun • Adm*
• www.gahoemuseum.org

Colorful pieces in the Gahoe Museum

Kukje Gallery
국제 갤러리

One of Seoul's most influential galleries, Kukje is the de facto local showcase for today's biggest global artists.

◈ *54 Samcheongno • Map L2 • 735 8449 • Open 10am–6pm Mon–Sat, 10am–5pm Sun • Adm • www.kukjegallery.com*

Embroidered items, Dong-Lim Knot Museum

Dong-Lim Knot Museum
동림매듭공방

Another museum located in a *hanok*, this one displays a variety of local knots, known as *maedeup*. The most interesting are the *norigae*, which feature on *hanbok*, Korea's national dress. ◈ *11–7 Gahoedong • Map M1 • 3673 2778 • Open 10am–6pm Tue–Sun • Adm*

Arario Gallery
아라리오갤러리

This small gallery with two exhibition rooms often showcases the works of Chinese artists.
◈ *149–2 Sogyeokdong • Map M2 • 723 6190 • Open 10am–7pm Tue–Sun*

6 Asian Art Museum
아시아 미술관

This fascinating gallery-cum-museum is located in the backstreets of Samcheongdong. A beautiful place, it has many charming displays and a highly photogenic exterior – remember to stop and take in the wonderful tiling on the wall. ◈ *35–91 Samcheongdong* • *Map D1* • *4876 0191* • *Open 10am–7pm Tue–Sun* • *Adm*

Mural tiles, Asian Art Museum

7 Hansangsoo Embroidery Museum
한상수 자수박물관

Located inside a beautiful *hanok*, this focuses on local embroidery. The admission fee includes a lesson in handkerchief-making. ◈ *11–32 Gahoedong* • *Map M1* • *744 1545* • *Open 10am–5pm Tue–Sun* • *Adm*

8 Buddhist Art Museum
불교 미술관

Dedicated to Buddhist art, this museum boasts almost 6,000 items. There are statues, copper bells, and scroll paintings, as well as ceramic objects featuring figures from Buddhism's pantheon of deities. ◈ *108–4 Wonseodong* • *Map N1* • *766 6000* • *Open 10am–5pm Mon–Sat* • *Adm*

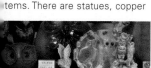

9 World Jewellery Museum
세계 보석 박물관

Tucked into the alleys above Samcheongdong, the World Jewellery Museum focuses, unsurprisingly, on jewelry from around the globe. There are amber pieces from the Baltic, metal crosses from Ethiopia, Egyptian headdresses, Parisian rings from the Art Nouveau era, and much more. ◈ *75–3 Hwadong* • *Map M1* • *730 1610* • *Open 11am–5pm Wed–Sun* • *Adm*

10 Owl Art & Craft Museum
올빼미 예술 공예 박물관

This is perhaps the most eccentric of the Bukchon area's many museums – at least since the closing of the Chicken Art Museum down the road. Whether they are embossed on a plate or vase, standing as figurines, or printed onto a postage stamp or a folding screen, you'll find over 2,000 owls here, hailing from across the globe. ◈ *27–21 Samcheongdong* • *Map D1* • *3210 2902* • *Open 10am–7pm Thu–Sun* • *Adm*

Owl Art & Craft Museum

⑩ Gwacheon 과천

Seoul is one of the most densely populated cities in the world – over 25 million people live in the city and its catchment area. With parkland at a premium here, travelers staying for longer than a few days might wish to escape the crowds and enjoy some pristine greenery. The neighboring city of Gwacheon makes the perfect destination; it is centered on Seoul Grand Park, a large, mountain-backed swath of land which also boasts a superb gallery, a huge zoo, and one of Korea's biggest theme parks.

Scale model of Cheonggyesan mountain

🌟 Seoul Grand Park and Seoul Land are popular retreats. For a little peace and quiet, come early in the day or late in the afternoon.

🛍 There are many shops selling snacks in and around Seoul Land and Seoul Grand Park. For long hikes, carry water and snacks with you.

• Map G2
• National Museum of Contemporary Art: Open Mar–Oct: 9am–6pm Tue–Sun, Nov–Feb: 10am–5pm Tue–Sun; Adm
• Seoul Grand Park & Zoo: Open Mar–Oct: 9am–7pm daily, Nov–Feb: 9am–6pm daily; Adm: W3,000 (Seoul Zoo)
• Gwacheon National Science Museum: Open 9:30am–6pm Tue–Sun; Adm: W4,000; www.scientorium.go.kr • Seoul Land: Open 9:30am daily, closing time varies from 6 to 10pm; Adm: W18,000 (day-pass W32,000); www.eng.seoulland.co.kr

Top 10 Features

1. National Museum of Contemporary Art
2. Seoul Grand Park
3. Seoul Zoo
4. Cheonggyesan
5. Gwacheon National Science Museum
6. Seoul Race Park
7. Equine Museum
8. Seoul Land
9. Gwacheon Hyanggyo
10. Gwanaksan

National Museum of Contemporary Art
Affiliated to the eponymous facility in Deoksugung palace *(see p75)*, this museum owns over 8,000 artworks from Korea and abroad.

Seoul Grand Park
This gigantic green area, centered on a lake *(above)*, spreads up into the surrounding mountains. In good weather, you could spend the whole day here.

Cheonggyesan
This mountain lies to the back of Seoul Grand Park and some of its many hiking trails start in the park itself. Hiking enthusiasts can try scaling the 2,027-ft (618-m) high summit.

Seoul Zoo
A part of Seoul Grand Park, this is one of Asia's largest zoos *(right)*. It is home to animals such as zebras and giraffes, and there is also a petting zoo.

 A Cultural Street Festival takes place near Gwacheon station every Saturday from April to October.

5 Gwacheon National Science Museum

Most museums focus on past discoveries but exhibitions here are quite futuristic *(left)*. There is also a planetarium and, outside, a sculpture-studded walking space.

6 Seoul Race Park

This race park *(above)* is one of the only places in South Korea where gambling is legal. Races take place from 10am to 5pm on weekends and you can also bet on horses running in Jeju and Busan – the only other courses in the country.

7 Equine Museum

This small museum inside the Race Park complex is dedicated to horses and has a number of horse-centric paintings and sculptures.

8 Seoul Land

A huge amusement park *(main image)*, Seoul Land has over 40 rides – the Sky-X, a 180-ft (55-m) high affair, is the most famous. The complex also has a series of mock-European buildings and walking trails.

Betting and Gambling in Seoul

The Seoul Race Park in Gwacheon is one of the few places in South Korea where it is legal for locals to gamble. However, plenty of small-scale betting takes place in other forms, the most popular of which is a local card game known as *hwatu* – older Koreans can often be spotted playing this game outdoors. The small, decorative cards used to play *hwatu* can be purchased from any convenience store, and they also make great souvenirs.

9 Gwacheon Hyanggyo

In the dynastic era, aristocrats studied at Confucian academies known as *hyanggyo*. This one *(above)* lies in the foothills of Gwanaksan.

10 Gwanaksan

Rising up to the west of Gwacheon, this small mountain has many hiking trails. The easy 90-minute walk up to the 2,073-ft (632-m) summit is recommended.

Left **World Peace Gate, Seoul Olympic Park** Right **FIFA World Cup semifinal 2002, Seoul**

🔟 Moments in History

1 18 BC: Founding of Baekje

King Onjo founded the Baekje dynasty, one of Korea's famed Three Kingdoms. Though the exact location of Wiryeseong, Baekje's first capital, remains unknown, experts agree that it lay within the boundaries of present-day Seoul – most likely near what is now Jamsil.

2 1394: Seoul Becomes a Capital

King Taejo made Seoul the first capital of Joseon (1392–1897), a dynasty he had founded two years earlier. His influence is still felt today – the palace of Gyeongbokgung was built within a decade, as were much of the city walls and their colossal gates.

Gyeongbokgung

3 1450: Death of King Sejong

King Sejong's main legacy was *hangeul*, the Korean alphabet – invented during his reign as a means of enabling the education of the common man. However,

widespread literacy was only achieved by the 20th century. To this day, Sejong is revered as one of Korea's greatest leaders.

4 1590s: Japanese Invasions

This decade saw two major invasions of Korea by Japanese armies, led by General Hideyoshi. Most of the fighting took place on Korea's southern coast, though much of Seoul was also destroyed in the process.

General Hideyoshi

5 1762: Murder of Prince Sado

This royal murder occurred in Changgyeonggung, when, at the behest of King Yeongjo, Prince Sado – his son and heir to the Joseon throne – was left to die inside a rice casket.

6 1910: Japanese Annexation

After Japan formally annexed Korea in 1910, systematic attempts to eradicate Korean identity were made (including the renaming of Seoul as "Keijo" until Japan was forced from power at the end of World War II

Preceding pages **Serene Hyangwon Pavilion, Gyeongbokgung palace**

Han river bridge, destroyed in the 1950 war

1950: Korean War

Following the war, Korea was divided into a Soviet-backed north and a Western-backed south. The inevitable civil war kicked off in 1950, with Seoul changing hands four times before the 1953 armistice. A peace treaty has not been signed yet.

1962: Park Chung-hee Takes Control of Korea

Military strongman Park Chung-hee seized power of South Korea in a *coup d'état*, and officially became president the next year. Though often authoritarian, Park's rule saw the country develop from a war-scarred backwater into an industrial powerhouse.

1988: Seoul Olympics

Although the Summer Games held in Seoul were a success, some of the most memorable moments were quite unusual: doves burning to death on the lighting of the torch; Ben Johnson's 100m world record and subsequent disqualification; and Greg Luganis winning the diving gold medal after hitting his head on the board.

2002: FIFA World Cup

Seoul hosted the opening game of football's World Cup, an event co-hosted with Japan. South Korea became the first Asian country to play in the World Cup semifinals, and was defeated by Germany, who won 1-0.

Top 10 Kings of Joseon

1 Taejo (1392–98)
Founder of the Joseon Kingdom, he helped shape today's Seoul with a series of grandiose projects.

2 Taejeong (1400–1418)
Taejo's fifth son inherited the throne after murdering or exiling other contenders, including his own siblings.

3 Sejong the Great (1418–50)
Revered king who ushered in an age of invention, including the Korean alphabet.

4 Seongjong (1469–94)
This king continued Sejong's legacy by encouraging invention and experimentation.

5 Yeonsangun (1494–1506)
Notorious tyrant who launched purges of intellectuals. His love for a male court jester was portrayed in the 2005 film *The King and the Clown*.

6 Seonjo (1567–1608)
Infamous for not protecting the country during the 1590s, Seonjo even had the eventual savior, Admiral Yi Sun-shin, arrested and tortured.

7 Sukjong (1674–1720)
Amid factional infighting, Sukjong still managed to enhance Joseon's prosperity.

8 Jeongjo (1776–1800)
The son of Prince Sado *(see p34)*, he reformed Joseon in a turbulent period.

9 Gojong (1863–1907)
Crowned king as a child, first Gojong's father, and then eventually, his consort ruled the country on his behalf.

10 Sunjong (1907–10)
The final king of Joseon, whose rule ended with Japan's annexation of the country.

Left **Cherry blossoms at Yeouido** Right **Dancers at the Seoul Drum Festival**

🔟 Festivals and Events

Cherry Blossom Season
Spring heralds the cherry blossom season, with gorgeous blossoms weighing down the city's many cherry trees. Yeouido's riverfront is the standard viewing area for Seoulites, though those in the know make a beeline for the less crowded Seoul Grand Park (see p30). ◈ *Usually Apr*

International Women's Film Festival
This film festival, held each year in Seoul, screens movies, documentaries, and short works by famous and independent women filmmakers from across the globe. ◈ *Mid Apr • www.wffis.or.kr*

Lotus Lantern Festival
Buddha's birthday sees Seoul's various temples decorated with thousands of colorful lanterns – a sight

Giant lantern, Lotus Lantern Festival

just as spectacular by night as it is by day. Jogyesa temple (see p10) is the hub of proceedings, though the mountains of Bukhansan National Park (see pp22–3), which is home to several temples, offer a more relaxing experience. ◈ *May*

Jongmyo Daejae
The kings of the Joseon dynasty (1392–1910) venerated their ancestors five times a year at the Jongmyo shrines (see p21). Though Korean royalty has long faded into history, the spectacular ceremony is re-enacted each spring, and it is one of the most traditional and beautiful events in Seoul's calendar. ◈ *1st Sun in May*

Jisan Valley and Pentaport Rock Festivals
Seoul's two main rock festivals take place simultaneously at separate venues just outside the city. Japan's Fuji Rock takes place at almost the same time, bringing quite a few big international groups to the area. ◈ *Late Jul • Jisan Valley: www. valleyrockfestival.mnet.com • Pentaport: www.pentaportrock.com*

Seoul Plaza Events
Free musical performances, many traditionally Korean in nature, take place each summer evening on Seoul Plaza. ◈ *Map L5 • Throughout summer*

7 Seoul Open Night

This is a night of performances throughout the city, with free shuttle buses that ferry revelers between the venues. Certain Seoul sights, including some palaces, are opened up until midnight – an annual opportunity to see them under cover of nighttime. ◐ *Aug*

8 Seoul Drum Festival

A mix of international and local drumming ensembles feature at this event, known for encouraging audience participation. Even if you're not hauled onstage to embarrass yourself in front of a crowd, you'll be able to take lessons in playing traditional Korean drums. ◐ *Late Sep • www.seouldrum.or.kr*

Fireworks Festival

9 Fireworks Festival

The most explosive event of the year – in at least one sense – takes place on Yeouido's riverfront. It is hugely popular, so arrive early to ensure viewing space. ◐ *Early Oct • www.bulnori.com*

10 Seoul Performing Arts Festival

Seoul has fantastic performances throughout the year, but SPAF is a particular highlight, showcasing an eclectic range of local and international troupes. Venues are spread around the Daehangno area. ◐ *Oct • www.spaf21.com*

Top 10 Holidays

1 Jan 1, New Year's Day
New Year's Day sees Seoulites partying, with City Hall as the focal point.

2 Mar 1, Independence Day
With flags galore, South Korea commemorates the 1919 movement against Japanese annexation. A reading of the Declaration of Independence takes place in Tapgol Park.

3 Mar 14, White Day
Though not a national holiday, White Day sees girls buying gifts for their men, a month after Valentine's Day.

4 May 5, Children's Day
Parents take their children to amusement parks or zoos for a day of fun and games.

5 Apr/May, Buddha's Birthday
Seoul's temples and streets are strewn with lanterns celebrating Buddha's birthday.

6 Jun 6, Memorial Day
A commemoration of those who died in service or in the independence movement.

7 Aug 15, Liberation Day
The day of the Allied victory over Japan, which resulted in Korea's independence.

8 Oct 3, National Foundation Day
Celebrates the founding of the first Korean state in 2333 BC by the legendary God-king Dangun.

9 Nov 11, Pepero Day
This is not a national holiday, but sees convenience stores crammed with Koreans buying their loved ones Pepero chocolate sticks.

10 Dec 25, Christmas Day
Christmas is observed as a national holiday in Korea.

Left **City model, Seoul Museum of History** Right **Seoul Museum of Art**

Museums and Galleries

1 Leeum, Samsung Museum of Art

리움, 삼성 미술관

This gallery is split into two main halls designed by architects Mario Botta and Jean Nouvel. One houses several forms of traditional Korean art, while the other features contemporary works from Korea and abroad *(see p85)*.

2 Kukje Gallery

국제 갤러리

With a name like Kukje – Korean for international – it is easy to guess what this gallery focuses on. Since its opening in 1982, Kukje gallery has been showcasing works by well-known artists such as Joseph Beuys, Damien Hirst, and Cy Twombly, as well as helping popularize Korean art overseas *(see p28)*.

Bronze bell, National Museum of Korea

3 National Museum of Contemporary Art

국립 현대 미술관

This museum has two superb locations – a colonial-era structure in Deoksugung palace *(see p75)*, and the the leafy surroundings of the Seoul Grand Park *(see p30)*. Head to the former if pressed for time, and the latter for a day trip *(see p76)*.

4 National Museum of Korea

국립 중앙박물관

Korea's flagship museum of history and art is spread over three large floors, each with a certain theme. The first floor has exhibits dating back to the Three Kingdoms period and beyond, the second focuses on paintings and calligraphy, and the third holds pottery and Buddhist sculptures *(see pp14–15)*.

National Museum of Contemporary Art

Entrance of the Owl Art & Craft Museum

Owl Art & Craft Museum
올빼미 예술 공예 박물관
Displays here include sculptures, figurines, and paintings of owls; the museum is truly representative of the Bukchon area's quirky galleries *(see p29)*.

Gana Art Gallery
가나 아트 갤러리
Designed by Jean-Michel Wilmotte, the same architect responsible for the award-winning Incheon International airport, this extensive gallery displays a variety of exhibits. Visitors can view paintings, video art, and more in a single afternoon *(see p24)*.

National Palace Museum of Korea
국립 고궁박물관
Located in the Gyeongbokgung palace grounds and accessible on the same ticket, this museum exhibits an assortment of stonework, calligraphic scrolls, painted eaves, and other treasures from Seoul's five palaces *(see p9)*.

Whanki Art Gallery
환기미술관
This gallery is dedicated to the works of Kim Whanki, a famous abstract artist whose work was inspired by the three cities he lived in – Seoul, Tokyo, and Paris. It also organizes exhibitions featuring similar work by contemporary Korean artists *(see p24)*.

Seoul Museum of History
서울시립미술관
The collections in this museum not only give a glimpse of the Seoul of the past, but an understanding of its transformation into a world-class city. It also hosts art exhibitions from time to time *(see p76)*.

Seoul Museum of Art
서울시립미술관
This building once housed the Supreme Court of Korea. Remodeled in 1995, the gallery has exhibited works of masters such as Mark Rothko, Henri Matisse, and Vincent van Gogh, and its modern interior is suitably splendid *(see p76)*.

Left **Interior of Samsung D'light** Right **Incheon International Airport**

Modern Seoul

The glass facade of the Jongno Tower

1 Jongno Tower
Seoul's metamorphosis from the Brutalist designs of the 1980s can be said to have started with the renovation of Jongno Tower in 1999. Uruguayan architect Rafael Viñoly endowed what had been a simple tower block with an eye-catching "floating platform," supported by three latticed columns. ❧ 4 Jongro 2-ga • Map M4

2 SK Building
Impressive as the Jongno Tower renovation was, it offered little insight into Seoul's future layout. SK Building, on the other hand, caused little fuss when completed a year later, but has since gone on to become the city's architectural reference point – many newer neighbors have aped its wonky steel-and-glass approach. ❧ 11 Eulji-ro 2-ga • Map L4

3 Incheon International Airport
Incheon International Airport, opened in 2001, proved a vast improvement on its functional predecessor, Gimpo Airport. All flowing lines, gentle curves, and open spaces, it has gone on to scoop a whole host of international airport awards. ❧ 2851 Unseodong, Incheon • Map F2

4 Cheonggyecheon
The renovation of the Cheonggyecheon stream, completed in 2005, involved tearing up the elevated highway and market areas which had covered the stream for decades. Seoulites expressed deep concerns at the cost – but millions pop by each year for a walk by the stream. ❧ Map M4

Walking along the Cheonggyecheon stream

5 Times Square and D Cube City
Created in an effort to revitalize the city's southwestern corner, these two projects are, perhaps, a sign of Seoul to come – a mix of office space, malls, parkland, bars, and restaurants, each topped with

The artificial floating islands in the Hangang river

a five-star hotel. ✆ *Times Square: 442 Youngdeungpodong 4-ga; Map A5 • D Cube City: 662 Gyeonginro; Map A5*

6 Floating Islands
"Floating" in the Hangang, these three artificial islands opened for business in 2011. Although primarily built to house conventions, performance venues, restaurants, and the like, their park areas are open to the public and are great for a stroll. ✆ *Map D5 • www.floatingisland.com*

7 Samsung D'light
Not all signs of modernity are architectural – take Samsung, a Korean company which has revolutionized television and mobile phone design. While you will see the latter in the hands of most of your fellow subway passengers, you can also take a peek at Samsung designs of the future in D'light, Samsung's electronics wing's superb showroom in Gangnam district. ✆ *1F & 2F 1320–10 Seocho 2-dong • Map E6*

8 City Hall
Completed in 2012, Seoul's new City Hall sits proudly at the center of the city, side-by-side with its Japanese-designed predecessor. Although said to resemble the

shape of temple eaves in design, the new building, soaring above the old, seems rather menacing in appearance. ✆ *Map L5*

9 New Districts
Seoul has made a habit of ripping up whole swaths of the city for the sake of modernization. A few areas have become quite spectacular – witness the ultra-modern surroundings of Gangnam station, or the even newer districts going up in Yongsan and Incheon's Songdo island.

10 Dongdaemun Design Plaza & Culture Park
Designed by Iraqi-born architect Zaha Hadid, this huge complex was built on the site of an old baseball stadium – and, evidently, a Joseon-dynasty garrison, remnants of which form part of a museum added to the original designs. ✆ *Map D2 • www.ddp.seoul.go.kr/eng/*

Dongdaemun Design Plaza & Culture Park

Left **Diners at Noryangjin fish market** Center **Making hoddeok** Right **Bulgogi, served with rice**

🔟 Culinary Specialties

1 Bibimbap
Literally meaning "mixed rice," this simple dish has religious origins, with the main ingredients of the dish corresponding to the colors linked with Buddhism locally – white for rice, yellow for egg, red for spice, green for vegetables, and blue for meat.

2 Barbecued Meat
Cooking your own meal in a restaurant may sound like a chore, but in Korea it's a lot of fun. Meat houses, called *gogi-jip*, dole out rounds of meat to customers, who finish the job on charcoal fires set into the tables. The most popular meats include *galbi* (marinated beef or pork ribs) and *samgyeopsal* (pork belly), and all are served with free side dishes.

3 Jeon
Korean pancakes, or *jeon*, come in many varieties. The most common are *bindaeddeok*

(mung-bean), *gamja jeon* (fried potato patties), and *haemul pajeon* (seafood).

4 Kimchi
The outside world might think of *kimchi* as Korea's national dish, although in reality, it is only a side dish. You will, however, get a small bowl with every local meal. This array of fermented vegetables comes in many forms, with spicy lettuce leaves and radish cubes as the most common.

5 Hanjeongsik
A must-try for those visiting Korea, these are traditional meals in which the whole table is blanketed with dozens of side dishes: a colorful mix of vegetables, meats, and fish served with rice, broth, and more.

6 Gimbap
Often referred to by Westerners as "California Rolls," *gimbap* are cylindrical rolls of rice *(bap)* wrapped in layered seaweed *(gim)*. Fillings always include egg and radish, with beef, salad, and tuna among the optional extras – you'll find them on sale at cheap chain eateries such as Gimbap Cheonguk and Gimbap Nara, found all over the city.

Cooking *jeon* at a food stall

Naengmyeon
7 A cold but spicy dish made with buckwheat noodles, *naengmyeon* is similar to Japanese *soba*. It's actually a North Korean specialty; many of Seoul's best *naengmyeon* restaurants, including Woo Lae Oak *(p46)*, were started by northerners who crossed the border during the Korean War.

Samgyetang
8 This delicious broth is made with ginseng-stuffed chicken, and is healthy even by the sky-high standards of Korean cuisine.

Samgyetang

Seafood
9 Korea's excellent seafood could have a whole book dedicated to it, but unfamiliarity makes most foreigners wary of trying it. The solution: head to Noryangjin Fisheries Wholesale Market *(p92)*, point at what you want, then take it up to an upper-floor restaurant, where your purchase will be prepared for you.

Hoddeok
10 For dessert, try to track down some *hoddeok* – small, rice-paste pancakes filled with brown sugar and ground nuts, then fried. In warmer months these treats can be tricky to find, though a few places on Insadonggil serve them year-round.

Top 10 Korean Staple Meals

Yokhoe
1 Pronounced "yook-hey", this dish is made with raw, minced beef, and topped with slices of Korean pear, sesame seeds, and a raw egg.

Ojingeo Deop-bap
2 If you like Korean spice, give this zingy little dish – chili-smothered squid *(ojingeo)* on rice *(bap)* – a try.

Bulgogi Deop-bap
3 This dish – marinated beef on rice – is one of the few Korean dishes that involves no red pepper paste whatsoever.

Doenjang Jjigae
4 A spicy soybean broth filled with goodies such as shellfish, strips of squid, and blocks of tofu.

Donggaseu
5 Pronounced "donk ass", this fried slice of breaded pork is smothered in a sweet sauce.

Bokkeumbap
6 Literally "fried rice," this dish comes most commonly as a simple combination of seasoned rice, flecks of meat, and a fried egg.

Mandu
7 These are dumplings, mostly steamed. *Gogi mandu* (filled with ground beef), and *kimchi mandu* are most common.

Mandu Guk
8 In this dish, the *mandu* come in a peppery, clear soup.

Ddeokbokki
9 A dish of rice-cake chunks *(ddeok)* in a thick, and very spicy, red-pepper soup.

Ramyeon
10 Noodles served in a spicy soup with greens and an egg. Try the *chijeu ramyeon*, with a slice of processed cheese.

Left *Soju* bottles Right *Bokbunjaju*, made with raspberries

Korean Alcoholic Drinks

1 Makgeolli
A milky-colored, still-fermenting rice wine with the alcoholic strength of a strong beer, *makgeolli* has seen a huge surge in popularity in recent years. Once an "old man's drink" consumed at home or in restaurants, it's now a hit with local youth. Some bars in trendy Hongdae and Gangnam are devoted to the drink, though you can buy the main varieties at any convenience store.

Different brands of *makgeolli*

2 Baekseju
This nutty, wine-strength brew is made with ginseng, cinnamon, ginger, and other healthy ingredients. In fact, its name means "100-year alcohol," since it's supposed to elongate your life span. True or not, Baekseju is a tasty beverage, and one often consumed in restaurants alongside barbecued meat. You can also try it in draught form at Baekseju Maeul (see p83).

3 Bokbunjaju
Made with mountain berries, *bokbunjaju* is a very sweet, deep purple wine. While all convenience stores sell it in factory-made form, there's no substitute for the real deal, sold near the entrances to Bukhansan National Park (see pp22–3) during fall.

4 Maehwasu
This sugary Baekseju-like traditional drink is made with the flower of the *maesil* – a kind of Korean green plum. Maehwasu is available in convenience stores and some restaurants.

5 Dongdongju
Very similar to *makgeolli*, but slightly thicker – in fact, a different end-product of the same process – *dongdongju* is sold by the bowl in most restaurants selling Korean pancakes known as *jeon*. Bars selling *dongdongju* tend to serve it in metal kettles – look for them on the street-sides in student areas.

6 Maesilju
Made, like Maehwasu, with *maesil*, this is a tart, sugary drink sold in convenience stores and some of the more traditional restaurants.

7 Yakju
The term *yakju* means "medicinal alcohol." Tastes and strengths vary, but one popular variety is Dandelion

Daepo, made with dandelion and sold in some restaurants that serve barbecued meat.

Ceramic *soju* bottles

8 Soju

The official national drink, *soju* is traditionally made with sweet potato, though these days cost-cutting means that the end result can often taste markedly chemical. It is sold in all convenience stores, as well as in every bar and most restaurants, and thrown back shot-style.

9 Wine

Korean wine, with its peculiar taste, is not for the faint-hearted. Majuang, sold in supermarkets, is the main local brand. Even more unusual is Jinro House Wine, an almost pop-like drink made with grape juice and *soju*, and sold in all convenience stores.

Korea Red ginseng wine

10 Beer

Korea's beer isn't much better than its wine, but the main brands – OB, Cass, and Hite – are cheap and available everywhere, often in draught form.

Top 10 Makgeolli Brands

1 Seoul Makgeolli
A light, slightly fizzy drink, this is the nation's number one brand.

2 Uri Haepsallo Bizeun Uguksaeng Makgeolli
Slightly sparkling with a creamy taste, this is an offering from the Guksundang conglomerate.

3 Ssal Guksundang Makgeolli
Another Guksundang brew, this is a heavy, flat *makgeolli* with an almost caramel-like taste.

4 Gongju Bam Makgeolli
Although its chestnut flavoring is artificial, this is a very tasty drink.

5 Sobaeksan Geomeunkong Makgeolli
You may have to travel to Danyang *(see p62)* to get this, but it's worth it – it may be the country's tastiest variety of black-bean *makgeolli*.

6 Soony Makgeolli
This popular *makgeolli* has a light, fresh taste.

7 Urisal Tokssoneun Ssal Makgeolli
A crisp, almost apple-like taste makes this a real winner.

8 Horangi Makgeolli
This pricey "Tiger" *makgeolli* is a favorite with connoisseurs.

9 Urisul Bokbunja Makgeolli
Made with mountain berries, this is a popular flavor, and one of the easiest fruit *makgeollis* to track down.

10 Ihwaju
Rare and delicious, this one is stronger and more viscous than the regular offerings.

A convenience store is always close by in Seoul – 7-Eleven, CU, GS25, and Buy the Way are the major chains.

45

Left **Desserts at OKitchen** Center **Wine Cellar, Jung Sikdang** Right **Entrance of Doore restaurant**

🔟 Restaurants

1 Balwoo Gongyang
발우공양

In any other developed country, the exquisitely prepared food at Balwoo Gongyang would cost a small fortune. This restaurant is operated by monks from Jogyesa, Seoul's main Buddhist temple *(see p10)*. The set meals are highly recommended, and guests are guaranteed to be pleasantly surprised by the well-presented and delicious vegetarian cuisine served here *(see p11)*.

Woo Lae Oak

2 Woo Lae Oak 우래옥

One of Seoul's oldest restaurants, Woo Lae Oak was started by North Koreans in 1945, just before the outbreak of the Korean War. Now housed in a retro building, it's revered as the best place in South Korea to try North Korea's signature dish, *naengmyeon* – a bowl of cold buckwheat noodles served in a spicy soup *(mul naengmyeon)* or an even spicier paste *(bibim naengmyeon)*, and topped with a boiled egg and slices of Korean pear *(see p79)*.

3 Congdu Iyagi 콩두 이야기

A restaurant which serves "neo-Korean" cuisine, and overlooks the gardens of the Seoul Museum of History *(see p76)*. The menu here changes by the season, and they serve some rare Korean alcoholic drinks – try the *ihwaju (see p79)*.

4 Goongyeon 궁연

This restaurant serves banquet meals that are literally fit for a king. The creator of these dishes – Han Bok-ryeo – is the only person in the land with a direct link to royal court cuisine, and has long been designated a living national treasure *(see p101)*.

5 Min's Club 민스클럽

One of Seoul's most beautiful restaurants, Min's Club is also one of its most vaunted

Interior of Min's Club

for food and drink alike. Its menu has traditional Korean dishes as well as a smattering of French choices, such as sliced salmon gravlax with wasabi cream, marinated beef with flying-fish roe, or sautéed mushrooms with home-made ricotta *(see p71)*.

Doore 두레
Housed in a *hanok* abode built in the early 1900s, Doore serves delicious imitations of imperial-court cuisine. The interiors are decorated with scrolls and paintings, and the meals are served in beautiful handmade bowls and trays. The set meal here is a good option, though there's also an à la carte menu which features intriguing takes on the humble *bibimbap (see p71)*.

OKitchen 오키친
A *hanok* restaurant whose dishes are the brainchild of esteemed chef Susumu Yonaguni, who grows many ingredients himself on a farm outside Seoul. The sushi and pasta are quite superb, as are the desserts *(see p89)*.

Jung Sikdang 정식당
Overlooking Dosan Park, this modern restaurant is a local attempt at molecular gastronomy, and quite a successful one. It serves traditional dishes enlivened with foams, mousses, and distinctly non-Korean sauces *(see p101)*.

Gwangjang Market 광장 시장
Most of the dishes available in this zany market are on view,

Gwangjang Market

whether pre-cooked, part-cooked, awaiting the frying-pan or destined to be served raw. Among the most popular items are *bindaeddeok* – mung-bean pancakes – and *sannakji* – baby octopus tentacles *(see p16)*.

Pojangmacha 포장마차
Filled with plastic chairs and raucous locals, these tent-like restaurants are a quintessential Seoul experience – ramshackle affairs serving a variety of simple meals. There is no menu here; just point at what you like the look of and it will be prepared in no time *(see p71)*. Wash your meal down with some *soju* or *makgeolli (see pp44–5)*.

Left **Outdoor seating at Dawon** Right **Teas at Beautiful Tea Museum**

Tearooms

Suyeon Sanbang 수연산방
Most of the *hanok* tearooms in Insadong are re-creations of traditional abodes, but this is the real deal. A well-preserved wooden house, it was once the home of Sangheo, a noted local author, in the early 1940s. A dreamy place, whether you're sitting inside or out in the garden. ⊗ 248 Seongbukdong • Map D1 • 764 1736 • Open noon–10:30 pm daily

Yetchatjip 옛찻집
This tearoom's appeal lies in the small group of birds who use it as a kind of giant cage, zooming from perch to perch, bathing in the water fountains, or even fluttering onto your table for a closer look as you drink your tea. ⊗ 2–2 Gwanhundong • Map N3 • 722 5019 • Open 10am–10pm daily

Dalsae Neun Dal Man Saenggak Handa
달새는 달만생각
With a fanciful name meaning "Moon Birds Think Only of the Moon," this tearoom offers wonderful traditional brews in a secluded, faux-rustic setting. ⊗ 60 Gwanhundong • Map M3 • 720 6229 • Open 10am–9pm daily

Dalsae Neun Dal Man Saenggak Handa

Cha Masineun Tteul
차마시는뜰
Tucked into the side-streets of Bukchon Hanok Village *(see pp26–7)*, this structure dates from the early 1900s. They have a wide range of teas, and some tables offer wonderful views. ⊗ 35–169 Samcheongdong • Map L2 • 722 7006 • Open 10am–10pm daily

Cha Masineun Tteul

Suyoil 수요일
One of the older tearooms on Insadonggil, Insadong's main street, Suyoil boasts high ceilings and giant windows, but manages to retain a modern feel It is quite popular with young couples. ⊗ 23 Gwanhundong • Map M3 • 723 0191 • Open 10am–10pm daily

Margot 마르곧
An elegant tearoom with a traditional appearance, serving wonderful teas, all made from organic ingredients. ⊗ 129–5 Wonseodong • Map N1 • 747 3152 • Open 11am–10pm Tue–Sun

Dawon 다원
Forming part of the Kyungin art complex, in good weather it's hard to choose between Dawon's

outdoor tables and those in the beautiful indoor rooms. Note that if you choose the latter, you'll be sitting, in traditional fashion, on floor mats. 🔊 *30–1 Gwanhundong • Map M3 • 730 6305 • Open 10:30am–10:30pm daily*

8 **Gahwadang** 가화당
A tiny tearoom housed in a *hanok* building almost as old as the country itself – it dates back to the early years of Korean independence. Unlike most tearooms in the area, the focus here is firmly on green tea.
🔊 *35–103 Samcheongdong • Map D2 • 738 2460 • Open 11am–10pm Tue–Sun*

9 **Beautiful Tea Museum** 아름다운 차 박물관
Part museum, part shop, part school, and part tearoom, this is housed in a *hanok*-style building, though in decent weather visitors are advised to sit out in the charming courtyard.
🔊 *193–1 Insadong • Map A6 • 735 6678 • Open 10am–10pm daily*

Beautiful Tea Museum

10 **O'sulloc** 오설록
Korea's largest tea company, O'sulloc have a few tearooms in Seoul. Try the green teas: besides over a dozen grades of the regular brew, they offer green-tea latte, tiramisu, biscuits, and other delectable goodies.
🔊 *170 Gwanhundong • Map M3 • 732 6437 • Open 9am–10pm daily*

Top 10 Korean Teas

1 **Nok-cha**
Green tea, available in many different grades – though it can be hard to tell the difference unless you're a connoisseur.

2 **Saenggang-cha**
A highly popular winter-time drink, ginger tea is great if you feel a cold coming on.

3 **Daechu-cha**
Another winter warmer, this time made from the *daechu* – a kind of date also known as a *jujube*.

4 **Yuja-cha**
A citrus tea containing strips of peel, and often sweet-ened with honey or sugar.

5 **Omija-cha**
Even better ice-cold than hot, this lurid pink brew is made from the "five-flavored" *omija* berry.

6 **Maesil-cha**
Many Koreans make this slightly sour plum tea at home in the spring.

7 **Mogwa-cha**
Made with Chinese quince, this tea is often served in winter, when it's mixed with cinnamon.

8 **Bori-cha**
A simple barley tea that you might be served at res-taurants, alongside your meal.

9 **Insam-cha**
Tea made with ginseng, and served in a range of styles. The powder is a popular tourist purchase, particularly the healthy red ginseng variety known as *hongsam*.

10 **Ssanghwa-cha**
A bitter, deep brown concoction made from a number of medicinal herbs and revered for its healthy properties.

Left **A *hoddeok* at West 'n East** Center **Coffee beans at Club Espresso** Right **The Lounge**

🔟 Cafés

Café Madang

Café Madang 카페 마당
Located in the basement of the Hermés store in Apgujeong, the food in this café-cum-restaurant is pricey, but a cup of coffee is quite affordable – surprising, given the fact that your cup, the sugar spoon, and the table you're seated at will all be extremely expensive Hermés originals *(see p100)*.

Sanmotoonge 산모퉁이
This is one of Seoul's most delightful places to relax with a cup of coffee. Sanmotoonge's outdoor terrace provides vistas of Bukhansan National Park to the north, and the Seoul fortress walls to its east. It's also a fair uphill walk from the nearest public transport — a perfect opportunity to burn off some calories before you sit down for coffee and cake *(see p25)*.

Club Espresso 클럽 에스프레소
The ground floor of this café is a treasure trove of coffee beans from all over the globe. It is a popular place with expats – many of whom buy their coffee beans here. You can buy ready-made bags, or choose from dozens of varieties, many of which are ground to order *(see p73)*.

The Lounge 더라운지
This wonderful café-cum-restaurant is located in the Park Hyatt *(see p114)* and offers stunning views of Seoul. The smoothies, created by top sports nutritionist Patricia Teixeira, are highly recommended *(see p100)*.

Café aA 카페 aA
In student-filled Hongdae there's almost literally a café on every corner, and although there are many quirky establishments, few are truly unique. Step into Café aA, one of the most intriguing and distinctive cafés

Café aA

Interior, Books Cooks

in Seoul. The focus here is on furniture – there are two museum-like floors, featuring chairs by the likes of Salvador Dalí and Jean Prouvé. Those on the café floor are also miniature works of art *(see p95)*.

West 'n East 웨스트 엔 이스트
The first café in the land to realize the full potential of Korean desserts, West 'n East has given a new lease of life to the *hoddeok* pancake *(see p43)*. It serves excellent drinks as well, including many traditionally flavored takes on the humble latte *(see p100)*.

Doldamgil 돌담길
Don't miss the opportunity to drink coffee in Doldamgil *(see p83)*, which is located in the grounds of the Deoksugung palace. Not only are the views wonderful, but those

drinking coffee here will be aping history, as this is where King Gojong developed his own caffeine addiction.

Books Cooks 북스쿡스
Located in a renovated *hanok* abode, this café is a cozy, pleasantly dim venue in the winter, while in warmer months the ceiling is retracted, turning it into an airy courtyard. Their scones are scrumptious, and all handmade in front of you *(see p73)*.

74
The coffee at 74 is top-notch, and the establishment is quite superbly designed. Take a look at their drinks menu and you might want to head back for a designer martini in the evening *(see p100)*.

Hangang Bridge Cafés 한강 다리 카페들
The Hangang river splits Seoul into two, but up until recently, few restaurants or cafés offered decent views of this wide waterway. In 2009, the city government sponsored the creation of cafés on six Hangang bridges – they make great pit-stops if you're touring the south bank by bicycle.

Left **Signage outside Dduk Tak** Center **Patrons at Craftworks Taphouse** Right **Exterior of T-Lound**

🔟 Bars

1 Damotori 다모토리

One of the best *makgeolli* (see p44) bars in Seoul, Damotori offers over 30 varieties of the popular alcoholic drink. If you are trying *makgeolli* for the first time, order the sampler tray, which serves five different varieties in beautiful, handmade pieces of pottery. You will also be told the best order in which to drink them (see p88).

2 Dduk Tak 뚝딱

The focus of this Hongdae establishment is on different takes on rice wine, rather than the drink itself. Mixes made with fruit juice are the most popular – banana, kiwi, and strawberry are all highly recommended (see p94).

3 Baekseju Maeul 백세주마을

This restaurant-bar focuses on traditional Korean drinks with Baekseju (see p44) being its speciality. Other drinks are also available, including the

Diners at Baekseju Maeul

rare *ihwaju* – a deliciously gloopy *makgeolli*-like drink. Note that it is essential to order at least a little food here. Luckily, the *anju* (bar snacks) served are quite delectable. Give the *gamja jeon* (potato pancakes) a try (see p83).

Platoon Kunsthalle

4 Platoon Kunsthalle 플라톤 쿤스탄

A bar, a restaurant, an art gallery, and a performance space all rolled into one, this maverick establishment is housed inside a distinctive shell of shipping containers. The concept comes from Berlin, as do many of the beers and bar snacks. Catch a performance on weekend evenings (see p103).

5 T-Lound 티 라운지

A long-standing favorite, this lounge bar is a hip venue with three levels. The superb wine list here is often ignored in favor of the martinis, which are the main draw and are considered to be the best in Seoul (see p103).

Customers at a Korean bar are more or less obliged to buy food along with the drink.

Interior of Pierre's Bar

after Korean mountain ranges –
try the Geumgang Dark Ale,
the Namsan Pilsner, the Seorak
Oatmeal Stout, or the Jirisan
Moon Bear IPA *(see p88)*.

8 Ruf XXX 루프 XXX
Tucked into a side-street
that snakes up towards the
Namsan slopes, this bar exudes
a loungey vibe which is quite
at odds with the hectic nightlife
in the nearby district of Itaewon.
The rooftop terrace offers an
amazing view of Seoul, which
is best enjoyed with one of the
house cocktails *(see p88)*.

9 Club Evans 클럽 에반스
One of the best jazz bars
in the country, Club Evans is
located in Hongdae, which is
mostly popular with students.
It plays host to a couple of
sets each night – stay for both
and relax over a drink in
between *(see p94)*.

10 Ggot 쥐갓
Tucked into the basement
of an unassuming apartment
block, this small bar has live
music on weekends – usually
reggae. The cocktails here
are quite popular and there
are a few beer choices as
well *(see p94)*.

6 Pierre's Bar 피어리스 바
Located on the 35th
floor of the Lotte Hotel,
this swanky bar offers
stunning views of northern
Seoul. The extensive wine
list has personal selections
by well-known French chef
Pierre Gagnaire, and his
restaurant sits next door.
The bar also serves beer
and cocktails at reasonable
prices *(see p83)*.

7 Craftworks Taphouse
크래프트웍스 탭하우스
Microbrewed beers are slowly
gaining popularity in Seoul
and this bar has a decent variety
on offer. All beers are named

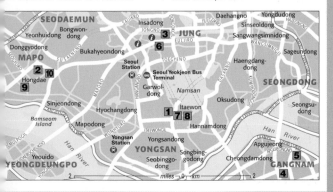

Left **Boon the Shop** Right **Ssamziegil sign**

Shops and Markets

A food stall at Gwangjang Market

Gwangjang Market
광장시장

There is fantastic food to be had at Gwangjang market, and though that's the major draw, there is also a range of shopping on offer. The fabrics are excellent – many top Korean designers source their material here – and there's a good selection of second-hand clothing on the second level of the market *(see p16)*.

Ssamziegil 쌈지길

This spiraling, modern market complex is one of the best places to buy souvenirs. There are dozens of outlets, and you'll find everything from bamboo earrings to fans made with mulberry paper. Given the market's popularity with tourists, prices are surprisingly fair *(see p11)*.

Yido Pottery
이도 도자기

Korea was once famed across Asia for its pottery. A trawl around this multilevel shop *(see p72)* makes it evident why its popularity remains. Yido features complete ranges from a number of artisans, most of whom learned their trade at Hongdae.

Galleria
갤러리아

If you're looking for designer clothing, head to Apgujeong's twin Galleria malls. The eastern wing is more luxurious, while the western wing has more Korean designers – and is a work of art in itself, paneled with scales of plastic that light up quite spectacularly at night *(see p102)*.

Bespoke Tailoring

Tailored clothing is excellent value in Seoul, with the Itaewon district particularly recommended for shirts and suits. The main road, Itaewonno, has many shops. Some are better than others, but it's easy to sort the wheat from the chaff.

Colorful products at Yido Pottery

Interior, Maison de Lee Young Hee

6 Maison de Lee Young Hee 이영희한복집

Few foreigners venture into the world of *hanbok*, Korea's traditional clothing. Though beautiful, the outfits are expensive and far too cumbersome for regular use. Lee Young Hee is the most famed of the few local designers to have incorporated *hanbok* styles into regular clothing, even counting Hillary Clinton as a customer at her New York City outlet *(see p102)*.

7 Boon the Shop 분 더 샵

This prestigious shop sells wares from most of Korea's top designers, as well as a selection from overseas. The exceptions are local menswear labels, which you'll find at a sister mall just down the road *(see p102)*.

8 Dongdaemun Market 동대문시장

The Dongdaemun area's many malls are Seoul's greatest shopping draws. Many visitors from Japan and other Asian nations weekend in South Korea for this purpose alone, and, given the incredible range of clothing on offer, it's easy to see why. The huge Doosan Tower is the largest of the malls, though Migliore and Hello apM aren't far behind *(see p16)*.

9 Yongsan Electronics Market 용산전자상가

South Korea is justly revered for its electronic goods, with the likes of Samsung, LG, and Daewoo all big players in the international market. The market areas stretching from Yongsan station specialize in electronic goods – to find the real bargains, take the pedestrian walkway across the train tracks.
🕙 *Hangangno 2-ga • Map C4*

10 Furniture

South Korea produces some wonderful, Oriental-style furniture, and some places sell genuine antiques from Joseon times: Tongin in Insadong is highly recommended. Far cheaper, however, are modern re-creations of dynastic-era styles. You'll find shops full of such items along the road north of Itaewon station. 🕙 *Tongin: 16 Gwanhundong • Map M3 • 733 4867*

Left *Makgeolli* Center *Kimchi* Right **Patient at Jaseng hospital**

TOP 10 **Healthy Seoul Experiences**

1 Jjimjilbang

Public baths, known as *jjimjilbang,* are located all over Seoul. A unique experience, these spas are surprisingly modern affairs – in addition to a series of gender-segregated pools and steam rooms, most of them boast small restaurants and Internet terminals, while quite a few have karaoke-style singing booths. Massage services are also available for an extra fee.

Green tea with ice cream

2 Tea

Although coffee now reigns supreme on Seoul's streets, tea is still the king of caffeine in Korean homes. Tearooms are plentiful in the charming neighborhood of Insadong *(see pp10–11 & pp50–51).* Local tea varieties of note include *saenggang-cha* (ginger tea), *daechu-cha* (date tea), *nok-cha* (standard green tea), as well as the shocking pink, five-flavored *omija-cha.*

Pine-floored interiors of the Guerlain Spa

3 Guerlain Spa

Located in the superb Shilla hotel *(see p114),* this excellent spa blends perfectly into its surroundings, with pine flooring augmenting the pine tree-lined slopes of Namsan outside. Simple facials or massages are available, though it's tempting to splurge on a full-day "experience package." Ⓢ *202 Jangchungdong • Map D3 • 2230 1167 • Open 7am–10pm daily*

4 Jaseng Hospital

In recent years, Seoul has been heavily promoted as a "health tourism" destination, because of the array of inexpensive, quality treatment centers located here. The Jaseng Hospital has a particularly stellar reputation – the treatment of spine and joint disorders is their forte. Ⓢ *635 Shinsadong • Map E4 • 3218 2167 • www.jaseng.net*

5 Kimchi

The variety of vegetable dishes known as *kimchi* are perhaps Korea's most famous culinary products *(see p42).*

Kimchi is loaded with nutrients and is easily available – it's included as a free side dish with almost every Korean meal.

Acupuncture

6 Outdoor Pools

Many higher-end hotels in Seoul have swimming facilities, but the outdoor pools that open up in summer are even more popular. The most accessible are in Yeouido and Ttukseom.
⊛ *Yeouido: 82–3 Yeouidodong; Map A4; Open Jul–Aug: 9am–8pm daily; Adm*
• *Ttukseom: 112 Jayang 3-dong; Map G4; Open Jul–Aug: 9am–8pm daily; Adm*

7 Makgeolli

In Korea, even alcoholic drinks can be healthy. The creamy rice-wine known as *makgeolli* is said to promote weight loss and lower cholesterol levels. Since it is still fermenting when the bottle is opened, it is claimed that one of these contains as much healthy bacteria as 100 pots of yogurt. However, the fact that it goes down so smoothly makes it easy to drink too much – watch out for the morning headaches *(see p44)*.

8 Oriental M...

Though m... what the West... traditionally te... "Oriental med... originated in C... is a great plac... such treatmen... tourist offices... can put you i... specialists offering a... and other therapies...

9 Korean Course...

Health and ban... rarely uttered in the... sentence, but Korea... known as *hanjeong*... possible to eat larg... of food without gai... Such banquets revolve around... rice, fish, and a soup, with these mains surrounded by over a dozen small – and mainly vegetarian – side dishes.

10 Hiking

Seoul is awash with hiking opportunities – the mountain of Namsan *(see pp18–19)* is central and has a number of delightful trails. However, if you have a little more time on your hands, a trip to Bukhansan National Park *(see pp22–3)* may be in order.

Hiking at Bukhansan National Park

Left **Lotte World** Right **A stream meandering through Bukhansan National Park**

🔟 Ways to Unwind

1 The Korea House 한국의 집
A wonderfully traditional experience, The Korea House comprises a restaurant offering a royal banquet and a performance hall showcasing *pansori* – a kind of Korean opera. Visitors can experience both in a single evening, and learn how to make Korean food as well *(see p79)*.

2 Lotte World 롯데 월드
The world's largest indoor theme park, Lotte World is the perfect place to spend a rainy day. The outdoor section has even more rides, and there is also a shopping mall, ice-skating rink, and folk museum in the complex *(see p98)*.

3 Seoul Grand Park
서울대공원
Just south of Central Seoul, this large area of parkland is ideal for a stroll. It is possible

Entrance to Lotte World

to spend a whole day here exploring its theme park, zoo, and one of Korea's best contemporary art galleries, the National Museum of Contemporary Art *(see p30)*.

View over the lake from Seoul Grand Park

4 Seoul Land 서울 랜드
Abutting Seoul Grand Park is Seoul Land theme park, one of Seoul's most popular attractions for those traveling with children *(see p31)*.

5 Excursions
Seoul is a densely populated place, so to unwind completely, consider a trip outside the city. There are many excellent excursion options, with Danyang, Nami Island, and Daecheon Beach among the most relaxing *(see pp62–3)*.

6 Templestay
Although Christianity has eclipsed Buddhism as South Korea's main religion, Buddhist temples still dot the land. It is possible to stay in many of them overnight – including several in

Seoul – as part of a Templestay program. Note that this means being up much before dawn.

Spa Therapy
There are few better ways to unwind than by heading to a spa such as Guerlain (see p58) or Dragon Hill Spa (see p86), or to the cheaper local alternatives – *jjimjilbang* (see p58).

Performance Arts
Seoul has a flourishing theater scene. You could stay here for a month and catch a different performance every single day – see the box for the best recommendations.

Coex Aquarium
코엑스 아쿠아리움
A large, sparkling aquarium with over 40,000 creatures, including penguins, seals, and all kinds of fish. There are some highly innovative display units – look for the bath tubs and toilet bowls (see p97).

Visitors at the Coex Aquarium

Bukhansan National Park
북한산 국립 공원
Comprising a series of pine-cloaked mountains, this national park plays host to many attractions, including the Bukhansanseong fortress. Take a stroll here, or, if you're feeling more energetic, try scaling one of the peaks (see pp22–3).

Top 10 Performance Arts and Venues

1 Nanta
A unique performance blending drumming and cookery. ✆ 739 8288 • nanta.i-pmc.co.kr

2 Miso
Korea's first musical, still going strong. ✆ 41 Chongdong-gil • Map K5 • 751 1500 • www.mct.or.kr

3 Drawing Show
Watch giant paintings being made on stage. ✆ 18–5 Chodong • Map P5 • 766 7848 • www.drawingtheater.com

4 The Korea House
Enjoy a traditional *pansori* performance after tucking into a royal feast (see p79).

5 Drumcat
An all-female drumming ensemble. ✆ 18–5 Chodong • Map P5 • 2274 2133 • www.drumcat.co.kr

6 Namsan Gugakdang
Beautiful venue staging a variety of traditional musical performances. ✆ 84–1 Pildong 2-ga • Map P6 • 2261 0500 • www.sejongpac.or.kr

7 Jump!
An entertaining martial-arts show which has made it to Broadway. ✆ 13 Donhwamun • Map N2 • 722 3995 • www.yegam.com

8 SPAF
The Seoul Performing Arts Festival is held each October, at venues across the city. ✆ 3668 0101 • www.spaf.or.kr

9 Seoul Plaza
Free open-air performances are held here each summer evening. ✆ Map L5

10 Daehangno
This student area is home to small theaters that showcase performances. ✆ Map Q3

Left **Demilitarized Zone sign at the border between North and South Korea** Right **Gongju**

🔟 Excursions from Seoul

1 Korean Folk Village
한국 민속촌

This charming re-creation of a Joseon-dynasty village offers a peek into the Korea of yesteryear. Dirt tracks weave between dozens of wooden houses, and traditional performances take place throughout the day. Though the "farmers' dance" is the undoubted highlight, look out for the Joseon wedding and the tightrope show. ✆ 107 Boradong, Yongin City • Map G2 • 031 288 0000 • Adm • www.koreanfolk.co.kr

A tightrope walker in the Korean Folk Village

2 Danyang 단양

A lakeside town, Danyang makes for an ideal getaway from the city – clean air, unhurried locals, and a relaxed pace of life. It's also a jump-off point for Guinsa, perhaps the most spectacular of Korea's many Buddhist temples, and a series of local caves. ✆ Map H2

Hwaseong fortress

3 The DMZ
비무장 지대

The Demilitarized Zone dividing North and South Korea may be one of the more dangerous borders on earth, but it is one of the most popular excursions for visitors to Seoul – you will find tour pamphlets in any hotel. Tours, which include the Joint Security Area (JSA), also offer the chance to step a few meters across the border under the eye of watchful – and armed – guards. ✆ Map F1 • www.koreadmztour.com/en/index.asp

4 Seongmodo 석모도

Of the hundreds of Korean islands that jut up from the Yellow Sea (known locally as the "West Sea"), Seongmodo is the most accessible from Seoul. The Buddhist temple of Bomunsa is the island's most vaunted sight, though some prefer to rent a bicycle and take off on the country roads. ✆ Map F1

5 Hwaseong 화성

This stunning fortress was built in the 1790s on the orders of King Yeongjo (see p35), and intended to be the hub of a new Korean capital. Now a UNESCO-listed site, the fortress walls make for a superb walk, affording views of Suwon, the modern city that sprung up around it. ✆ Map F2

A bridge at the park on Nami Island

Nami Island 남이섬

This small, tree-filled island found fame as a filming location in "Winter Sonata," a local drama series. The initial hordes of drama buffs have subsided, and the island's pristine pathways are now among the country's best places for a stroll. ◈ *Namiseom • Map G1 • 753 1247 • www.namisum.com*

Incheon 인천

Though most visitors to Korea arrive in Incheon, few see anything of the city itself – a pity, as its sights can easily fill half a day. Visit the gentrified Chinatown for a bowl of *jjajangmyeon* – noodles in black-bean sauce – before strolling up to Jayu Park for a view over the sea. ◈ *Map F2*

Daecheon Beach 대천 해수욕장

This area comes to life each July for Korea's wildest, dirtiest event, the Boryeong Mud Festival – carry spare clothing. At other times it's a great place to sample Korean seafood, and you can smother yourself in the famous local mud year-round at the Mud Center, a beachside spa. ◈ *Map F3*

Gongju 공주

A sleepy city, Gongju was the capital of the Baekje dynasty from 538 to 660. Evidence of this era still remains, most notably a series of royal burial mounds, and the thousands of pieces of golden jewelry that fill the local museum. A Baekje fortress, Gongsanseong, can also be visited here. ◈ *Map G3*

Jeongdongjin 정동진

Although a little far from Seoul, this east-coast village has some fascinating attractions. You can crawl around a North Korean submarine, which crashed off the coast in 1996, and an American warship that saw action in Vietnam and World War II. Look out for the ship-shaped Sun Cruise Hotel, perched precariously on a nearby cliff. ◈ *Map H1*

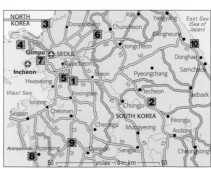

AROUND TOWN

SEOUL'S TOP 10

Left **King's living quarters, Changdeokgung Palace** Right **Lee Sang-Jae Memorial, Jongmyo Park**

The Palace Quarter

THE AREA AROUND SEOUL'S TWO OLDEST PALACES – *Gyeongbokgung and Changdeokgung* – offers a glimpse into South Korea's rich history. The palaces were built in the early 15th century, with the shrine of Jongmyo erected shortly afterwards. The Palace Quarter was at the helm of independence movements – the Seodaemun Prison is a relic of the Japanese annexation of 1910–45. After independence, Korea's first president moved into the Blue House behind Gyeongbokgung. Wooden buildings from those formative decades can be seen in Insadong and Bukchon Hanok Village – areas filled with shops, art galleries, and restaurants.

Gahoedong street, Bukchon Hanok Village

🔟 Sights

1. Gyeongbokgung
2. Changdeokgung
3. Bukchon Hanok Village
4. Bukhansan National Park
5. Insadong
6. Changgyeonggung
7. Buamdong
8. Jongmyo
9. Inwangsan
10. Seodaemun Prison History Hall

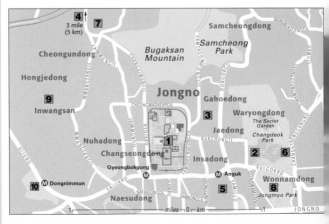

Preceding pages **A view of Seoul's skyline**

Throne Hall, Gyeongbokgung palace

1 Gyeongbokgung 경복궁
This splendid palace was built just after King Taejo (see p35) selected Seoul as the capital of his kingdom in 1392. Though spectacular today, history has not been kind to the palace – it was ravaged by fire twice in the 16th century and left in ruins for almost 300 years. Shortly after its restoration in 1888, Empress Myeongseong was assassinated here by Japanese agents. Japan formally annexed Seoul in 1910 and most of the buildings in the palace were destroyed once more. Carefully reconstructed, it is now perhaps South Korea's most popular tourist sight (see pp8–9).

2 Changdeokgung 창덕궁
A decade younger than Gyeongbokgung, and with a similar history, Changdeokgung is much better preserved – one reason behind its inclusion on UNESCO's World Heritage list. Certain artifacts here date back to the 1410s, most notably a small bridge named Geumcheongyo. At the rear end of the palace lie verdant grounds, with paths winding towards the revered "Secret Garden," which has a beautiful lake at its center (see pp20–21).

3 Bukchon Hanok Village 북촌 한옥 마을
Traditional Korean houses – wooden affairs known as hanok – are very hard to come by in modern Seoul. The Bukchon area, however, retains clutches of such abodes, arrayed along winding side-streets. Wander along these delightful streets and whichever way you go, you are sure to stumble across a quaint tearoom, a tiny gallery, or one of the many museums in the area (see pp26–9).

4 Bukhansan National Park 북한산 국립 공원
Few of the world's capitals can boast a national park in their catchment area, but Seoul is an exception. A popular spot, the park draws close to eight million visitors through the year. Though Central Seoul is just a few miles down the road, city life feels far away when walking on one of the trails in the park. The choice of activities is wide – visit one of over a dozen temples, go rock-climbing, or head to the granite peaks for a hike (see pp22–3).

View from Bukhansan National Park

Around Town – The Palace Quarter

Resilient Seoul

King Taejo made Seoul the capital of the fledgling Joseon dynasty in 1394. Given what the area has been through since then – the devastation by fire of two main palaces in the 1590s; the occupation of Korea by the Japanese (1910–45); and finally, the Korean War – it is astonishing that the original structures have remained in place.

Insadong 인사동
A popular tourist area, Insadong is markedly traditional by the standards of this resolutely modern city. Tiny side-streets meander off the main street, Insadonggil, and they boast a truly bewildering number of shops, tearooms, and galleries, almost all of which sell or display distinctive local fare. Sights around this area include Seoul's most important Buddhist temple, Jogyesa, and the city's unofficial sixth palace, Unhyeongung (see pp10–11).

Statue outside Jogyesa Temple, Insadong

Changgyeonggung 창경궁
The third major palace in the area, Changgyeonggung, though not as popular as the other two palaces, is considered by some to be the most

Blossoming cherry trees, Changgyeonggung

picturesque. Witness to a royal murder in 1762 (see p34), it is a surviving relic of the Japanese Empire's transformation of the palace into Korea's first theme park (see pp20–21).

Buamdong 부암동
Situated to the north of Gyeongbokgung palace, Buamdong, though relatively underdeveloped, has recently become extremely popular with young locals, who frequent the area's trendy cafés and restaurants. It also has two excellent galleries – Gana Art Gallery and the Whanki Gallery (see p24). Visitors with valid identification can now hike through Bugaksan, a mountain off-limits until recently, and still subject to high security surveillance (see pp24–5).

Jongmyo 종묘
Built during the rule of King Taejo, Jongmyo is a Confucian shrine (see p21). Ever since its construction, it has been used for the purpose of venerating Korea's royal ancestors – there were 27 kings in the Joseon dynasty alone, and following the Confucian code, each paid respects to his predecessors five times a year. Each May sees the Jongmyo Daejae, a colourful re-enactment of the ancient ceremonies (see p36).

Anguk (line 3), Jonggak (line 1) and Jongno 3-ga (lines 1, 3 and 5) are the most useful subway stations to get to the Palace Quarter.

9 Inwangsan 인왕산
Despite being suppressed by the Confucian aristocracy during the reign of the Joseon dynasty (1392–1910), shamanism remains part of Korean life to this day. Although their numbers are dwindling with each passing year, local shamanists have long considered the mountain of Inwangsan sacred, and it is here that you are most likely to see one of the spectacular practices pertaining to the creed. Religious fervor aside, the mountain's various paths, dotted with shamanic temples and shrines, are truly beautiful. ◈ Map C1

10 Seodaemun Prison History Hall 서대문 형무소
The most notorious prison in Seoul during Japan's annexation of Korea (1910–45), Seodaemun Prison is now a museum-cum-memorial, and highlights the atrocities committed here during the occupation. However, it remains tight-lipped on the fact that similar acts are widely considered to have been inflicted upon protesters well after independence. Here, it is easy to forget that South Korea was widely considered a dictatorship until the 1980s. ◈ 120–80 Hyeongeodong • Map C2 • Open Mar–Oct: 9:30am–6pm, Nov–Feb: 9:30am–5pm; closed Mon • Adm

Seodaemun Prison History Hall

A Day in the Palace Quarter

Morning

Begin your day with a cup of traditional Korean tea in one of Insadong's many excellent tearooms. **Yetchatjip** (see p10), with its friendly finches and canaries, is a long-standing favorite. From here you can take your pick of the area's three palaces – **Gyeongbokgung** (see pp8–9), **Changdeokgung** and **Changgyeonggung** (see pp20–21). All are superb sights, though given just a day, there's no real need to see all three. Spend the latter part of the morning getting pleasantly lost among the charming wooden abodes of **Bukchon Hanok Village** (see pp26–9), before stopping for coffee in trendy Samcheongdonggil.

Afternoon

Head back to Insadong for lunch – almost any of the area's restaurants are worth a visit. After lunch, take a leisurely walk around the area and browse any of its galleries or shops – the **Ssamziegil** complex (see p11) has dozens of stores selling souvenirs, while the **Sun Art Center** (see p70) and **Insa Art Center** (see p10) are the most vaunted repositories of art. If you have both time and energy left, head to **Jogyesa** temple (see p10) to experience Korean Buddhism in action. Insadong is, again, best for dinner, and for a nighttime stroll. The front courtyard of Gyeongbokgung is, however, the prime sunset spot, with the mountains behind the palace catching the last beams of the day rather beautifully.

Left **Fans on display, Insa Art Center** Center **Jongmyo Park** Right **Gwanghwamun Square**

Best of the Rest

1 Cheong Wa Dae 청와대

Hour-long tours of the official presidential abode and its superb gardens are available. Book online at least three weeks in advance, and bring your passport. ◎ *1 Cheongwadaero • Map C1 • 730 5800 • Tours at 10am, 11am, 2pm & 3pm Tue–Sat • www.english.president.go.kr*

2 Sun Art Center 선아트센터

One of Insadong's most prestigious galleries, Sun Art Center focuses on the work of Korean artists born before 1960. Inspired by the Korean War and Japanese occupation, the art is quite powerful. ◎ *184 Insadong • Map M3 • 734 0458 • Open 10am–6pm Mon–Sat • www.sungallery.co.kr*

3 Insa Art Center 선 아트센터

Look at original, contemporary art at this seven-floor gallery. The exhibitions change each week *(see p10)*.

4 Jogyesa 조계사

Seoul's most famous temple is the headquarters of the Jogye order, Korea's main Buddhist sect. There's also a Buddhist museum on site *(see p10)*.

5 Gwanghwamun Square 광화문 광장

Near Gyeongbokgung's famous south gate, this plaza features statues of two Korean heroes – Admiral Yi Sun-shin, who repelled the Japanese invasions of the 1590s, and King Sejong *(see p35)*, creator of the Korean alphabet. ◎ *Map L3*

6 Jongmyo Park 종묘공원

Outside the entrance to the Jongmyo Shrine is one of Seoul's most idiosyncratic sights. On sunny days, this small expanse of concrete is filled with elderly Korean men playing Chinese chess *(see p21)*.

7 Unhyeongung 운현궁

Often described as Seoul's sixth palace, Unhyeongung's charming wooden buildings are delightful to wander around in *(see p11)*.

8 Daehangno 대학로

This student area's main appeal is its range of small theaters. Although performances in English are rare, the shows can be quite a spectacle *(see p61)*.

9 Gilsangsa 길상사

Though a little difficult to find, this temple is less crowded and more beautiful than the Jogyesa complex *(see p10)*. ◎ *323 Seongbukdong • Map D1 • 3672 5945*

10 Seongnagwon 성낙원

This is one of South Korea's prettiest gardens, though tricky access and irregular opening hours mean there are few visitors. ◎ *Map D1*

Price Categories

For the equivalent of a meal for two made up of a range of dishes, or one large dish, with half a bottle of wine.

W	under W10,000
WW	W10,000–20,000
WWW	W20,000–50,000
WWWW	W50,000–100,000
WWWWW	over W100,000

Left **Dishes at Nwijo**

Places to Eat

1 Balwoo Gongyang 발우공양
Vegetarian Buddhist food in a gorgeous restaurant overlooking Jogyesa temple. Reservations are essential *(see p11)*. ✆ *WWW*

2 Galbi Golmok 갈비 골목
A side-street with several rustic restaurants serving barbecued meat. As is usual with such places in Korea, you'll cook your own meal at the table. ✆ *164 Myodong • Map N3 • WW*

3 Jaha Sonmandoo 자하손만두
Try dumplings with fillings such as shiitake mushrooms and leek here. ✆ *245-2 Buamdong • Map C1 • 379 2648 • WW*

4 Doore 두레
This restaurant, located on a tiny side-street, offers traditional dishes with a contemporary edge. ✆ *8-7 Insadong • Map C2 • 732 2919 • WWWWW*

5 Min's Club 민스클럽
Located in a beautiful *hanok* building, Min's Club serves a mix of Korean and French food. This is also a great place for tea or wine *(see p11)*. ✆ *WWWWW*

6 Pojangmacha 포장마차
These tent-restaurants offer one of Seoul's most quirky dining experiences. Ordering is as simple as pointing at what you want. ✆ *WW*

7 Pureun Byeol 푸른별
A popular place serving dishes from the mountains of Gangwon province – try the spicy *deodeok* (bellflower root) and *bindaedeok* (mung-bean pancake). ✆ *118-15 Gwanhundong • Map M3 • 734 3095 • WW*

8 Nwijo 뉘조
Housed in a beautiful *hanok* building, this excellent restaurant serves a mix of Buddhist temple food and court cuisine. ✆ *84-13 Gwanhundong • Map M3 • 730 9311 • WWW*

9 Dudaemunjip 두대문집
Try Korean staples such as *bibimbap* as well meals like *ddeok galbi* (seasoned meat patties) here. ✆ *64 Gwanhundong • Map M3 • 737 0538 • WW*

10 Seokparang 석파랑
Located near the Buamdong area *(see pp24-5)*, this place offers banquet meals. ✆ *125 Hongjedong • 395 2500 • Map B1 • WWWWWW*

Left **Yido Pottery** Center **Display at Kwang Ju Yo** Right **Sheep sculptures outside Ssamziegil**

TOP 10 Places to Shop

1 Ssamziegil 쌈지길
A multilevel shopping complex, Ssamziegil has dozens of trinket shops. Almost all stores here sell distinctly Korean fare *(see p11)*.

2 Sami 사미
This tiny store sells an interesting array of women's clothing – rustic and traditionally Buddhist in appearance, with a contemporary edge. ◎ *182 Insadong • Map M3*

3 Lee Geon Maan 이건만
The ties, handbags, and purses of this label feature characters from the Korean alphabet as part of their design. ◎ *197–4 Gwanhundong • Map M3 • 733 8265*

4 Bizeun 빚은
A small store, Bizeun sells colorful rice cakes that make fascinating souvenirs. ◎ *37 Insadong • Map M4 • 738 1245*

5 Kwang Ju Yo 광주요
A renowned pottery brand housed in a beautiful store, offering superbly designed tea sets, bowls, vases, and more. ◎ *203 Gahoedong • Map M1 • 741 4801*

6 Yido Pottery 이도 도자기
This large shop is almost a museum of contemporary Korean pottery. The wares on sale are all from top local talents, yet many are very affordable. ◎ *10–6 Gahoedong • Map M1 • 722 0756*

7 Korea Culture & Design Foundation 한국문화디자인협회
This store sells nicer trinkets than most other shops in Insadong. It also has pottery, paper products, and more. ◎ *182–2 Gwanhundong • Map M3 • 733 9041*

8 Sorihana 소리하나
Sorihana sells a range of pendants and fans, as well as traditional silk wrappings known as *bojagi*. Also available here are silk ties with the Korean alphabet woven into abstract designs. ◎ *31 Gwanhundong • Map M3 • 738 8335*

9 Sowyen 쇼엔
The jewelry sold in Sowyen has a distinct East Asian edge. This branch also has a café. ◎ *149 Seosullagil • Map P2 • 546 2498*

10 Tongin Building 통인빌딩
Go hunting for antique furniture from the Joseon era on the upper floors of this Colonial-era building. ◎ *16 Gwanhundong • Map M3 • 733 4867*

Left **Counter at Books Cooks** Right **A variety of coffees at Club Espresso**

10 Bars and Cafés

1 Books Cooks 북스쿡스
This appealing café is part-traditional Korean house and part-English tearoom. A range of teas are available here, and delicious scones are baked to order. ◎ *177–4 Gahoedong • Map M1 • 743 4003*

2 LN 엘엔
A re-created *hanok*, LN is a great place to kick back over a coffee or tea after a hectic day of sightseeing. Note that you'll be sitting on the floor, Korean-style. ◎ *27–1 Hwadong • Map M1 • 722 3152*

3 Pureun Byeol 푸른별
More of a restaurant than a bar, Pureun Byeol is a delightful venue offering a range of home-made *makgeolli* cocktails *(see p71).*

4 Club Espresso 클럽 에스프레소
Many expatriates head to Buamdong for the sole purpose of visiting this café, which offers Seoul's best range of coffee beans. Visitors can also sample the resultant brews. ◎ *257–1 Buamdong • Map C1 • 764 8719*

5 Sanmotoonge 산모퉁이
A bit of an uphill trek from the nearest bus stop, Sanmotoonge is well worth the effort. The café's outdoor terraces offer amazing mountain views *(see p25).*

6 Millimeter Milligram 밀리미터 밀리그램
Also known as MMMG, this local chain selling cups, pencils, envelopes, and other novelties has a lovely café at this branch. ◎ *153 Angukdong • Map M2 • 3210 1604*

7 Remini's 레미니스
A small café-cum-bakery tucked into the charming streets of Bukchon Hanok Village *(see pp26–7).* Try one of the delectable desserts. ◎ *120–1 Gyedong • Map M2 • 3675 0406*

8 Dugahun 두가훈
Just across the road from Gyeongbokgung palace *(see pp8–9),* Dugahun offers one of the best selections of wines in the city. ◎ *109 Sagandong • Map L2 • 3210 2100*

9 La Cle 라 클레
In the 1980s, this basement bar was a hangout for anti-government protestors. It is now one of the city's best jazz venues – performances take place most evenings. ◎ *95–1 Samcheongdong • Map M1 • 734 7752*

10 The Second Best Place in Seoul
서울에서 둘째로 잘하는 집
Poking fun at Korea's obsession with superlatives, this venue is popular for its *patjuk* – a sweet red-bean porridge garnished with chestnuts and cinnamon. ◎ *28–21 Samcheongdong • Map D1 • 734 5302*

Left **Statues, Namsangol Hanok Village** Center **Deoksugung** Right **Dongdaemun Market**

Central Seoul

SEOUL'S CENTRAL DISTRICTS *are supremely businesslike in nature: a near unbroken swath of glassy skyscrapers loom over the streets all the way from City Hall to Dongdaemun, with the gaps in between, and occasionally below, filled with shops. Once you delve into the area, you will find some of Seoul's best sights – two palaces from the Joseon dynasty, museums and galleries, and a re-creation of a traditional village. There's also a small but impressive range of colonial-era buildings. Add to the mix superb restaurants and cafés, and you have a recipe for at least a few days' sightseeing.*

🔟 Sights

1. Cheonggyecheon
2. The Plateau
3. Dongdaemun
4. Deoksugung
5. National Museum of Contemporary Art
6. Seoul Museum of Art
7. Seoul Museum of History
8. Gyeonghuigung
9. Namsangol Hanok Village
10. Shinsegae Department Store

Interior of the National Museum of Contemporary Art

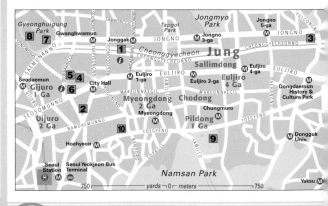

Cheonggyecheon stream

1 Cheonggyecheon 청계천
One of Seoul's most popular walking areas with locals and visitors alike, this stream attracted a huge amount of criticism on its opening in 2005 – a little peculiar, given that it is considerably more beautiful than the elevated highway it replaced. Construction costs aside, it's a stunner – and the streamside walkways stretch all the way to the Hangang (see p17).

2 The Plateau 플라토
Small but beautifully designed, this cultural venue was formerly known as the Rodin Gallery. Sculptures from the French master still feature in its main hall, the Glass Pavilion, which is illuminated almost entirely with natural light. Apart from Rodin's work, visitors can also see other pieces by local as well as foreign contemporary artists. ◈ 1F, Samsung Life Insurance Building, Taepyeongno 2-ga • Map K6 • 1577 7595 • Open 10am–6pm Tue–Sun • Adm • www.plateau.or.kr

3 Dongdaemun 동대문
A famous market space, this fascinating area is spread out both indoors and outdoors. It features a culture park designed by the acclaimed architect, Zaha Hadid, several intriguing streets on which Cyrillic text vies for supremacy with Korean, and the ancient city gate from which the district takes its name (see pp16–17).

4 Deoksugung 덕수궁
The palace of Deoksugung was first built in 1592, after Seoul's other palaces were burned down in the Japanese invasions. Much of its recent history also relates to Japan – King Gojong fled to this palace in 1897 after the assassination of his wife, and lived here for most of the period of Japanese occupation, during which two Neo-Classical buildings were erected. One of the buildings now houses the National Museum of Contemporary Art (see p76).
◈ 5–1 Jeongdong • Map K5 • 771 9952 • Open 9am–9pm Tue–Sun • Adm

Changing of the Guard, Deoksugung

Architecture in Central Seoul

Though the buildings of Central Seoul are almost entirely modern in nature, look a little closer and you will see that it also boasts fascinating specimens from previous centuries – Dongdaemun Gate and the palaces of Deoksugung and Gyeonghuigung, which are relics of the Joseon dynasty.

5 National Museum of Contemporary Art
국립 현대 미술관

Though this superb modern-art museum is a part of the Deoksugung palace (see p75), it is incongruously located in a Neo-Classical, Western-style building built in 1909 – evidence that the Joseon dynasty was opening up in its final years of rule. The exhibitions are always of a high standard, and tend to feature the works of local artists.
🔊 5–1 Jeongdong • Map K5 • 188 6000 • Open 9am–8:30pm Tue–Sun • Adm for special exhibitions • www.moca.go.kr

Central Atrium, Seoul Museum of Art

6 Seoul Museum of Art
서울시립미술관

Known as SeMA for short, this large, airy museum is the default Korean base for exhibiting works of famous international masters, past and present. There are usually two major exhibitions each year. Even the minor ones tend to be top-drawer, with Asian art and sculpture being the main focus. 🔊 37 Seosomundong • Map K5 • 124 8800 • Open 10am–8pm Tue–Fri, 10am–7pm Sat & Sun • Adm for special exhibitions • www.seoulmoa.org

Map of Seoul, Seoul Museum of History

7 Seoul Museum of History
서울역사박물관

This museum has a series of rooms showcasing artifacts from Seoul through the ages, as well as a "Development" section providing a window into how this fast-changing city will look in the future. There are frequent temporary exhibitions, and the permanent displays from the Joseon era are also well worth a visit.
🔊 Sinmunno 2-ga • Map J4 • 724 0274 • Open 9am–9pm Mon–Fri, 9am–7pm Sat & Sun • Adm for special exhibitions • www.museum.seoul.kr

8 Gyeonghuigung 경희궁
Although not as popular as the other five palaces in Seoul, Gyeonghuigung is nevertheless a truly gorgeous structure.

Although simpler in terms of layout than the other palaces, the paintwork here is stunning – head to the hill behind the palace for a great view.
⊛ 1–126 Sinmunno 2-ga • Map J3
• Open 9am–6pm Tue–Sun

9 Namsangol Hanok Village
남산골 한옥 마을
This re-created village, located on the slopes of Namsan (see pp18–19), provides a little trip back in time. Displayed here are five traditional *hanok* buildings – all dynastic-era structures pulled from other parts of the city. The buildings and their surrounding parkland make for a wonderful walk, especially in the evening when the area glows with strings of paper lanterns (see p19).

Hanok, Namsangol Hanok Village

10 Shinsegae Department Store 신세계 백화점
Built in 1930, this is the oldest of Korea's many department stores, and despite the presence of new stores such as Galleria (see p56), it is still the most beautiful – particularly when the Christmas decorations are up in December. Architecture aside, it is also a great place to shop for top Korean clothing and jewelry labels. ⊛ 52–50 Chungmuro 1-ga
Map L6 • 026 9000 • Open 10:30am–pm • www.shinsegae.com

A Day in Central Seoul

Morning

Central Seoul has a range of interesting options for your morning drink – have an espresso at the **Coffee Bean & Tea Leaf** (see p83), or tea surrounded by friendly cats at the **Goyangi Darakbang** (see p83). Try coffee with authentic Belgian chocolate at **Leonidas** (see p83), or a red-bean latte at **Gildeulyeojigi** (see p83). **Doldamgil** (see p83) is a little café inside the palace of **Deoksugung** – once home to King Gojong, a noted coffee addict, who had a special pavilion erected in which to enjoy his morning brew. Deoksugung also makes a great place to start the day's sightseeing – the **National Museum of Contemporary Art** forms part of the complex, while the even more impressive **Seoul Museum of Art** is just outside.

Afternoon

Stop for lunch at **Pierre Gagnaire à Séoul** (see p79) and then head to the streets of Myeongdong for an afternoon of shopping. If you are in the mood for some more sightseeing, hunt down **Shinsegae Department Store**, the **Former Russian Legation** (see p78), and other specimens of Japanese colonial architecture located nearby. In the evening, walk down to **Cheonggyecheon**, a stream whose beautiful subterranean paths form the best possible route to **Gwangjang Market** (see p16) – surely Seoul's most fascinating place for an evening meal and a cup of local rice wine.

Left **Bosingak** Center **A performance at Chongdong Theater** Right **Deoksugunggil street**

Best of the Rest

1 Namdaemun 남대문
First built in 1398, Seoul's beautiful "Great South Gate" was ravaged by fire following an arson attack in 2008. Its reconstruction is now underway. ✆ *29 Namdaemun 4-ga • Map C3*

2 Bosingak 보신각
Seoul's most important road was named after the bell that tolled in this belfry each evening, signaling the closure of the city gates and the beginning of the nighttime curfew. ✆ *Map M4*

3 Chongdong Theater 푸른별
This is the home of Miso, Korea's longest-running musical. Even if you're not here for a performance, head to Gildeulyeojigi, the on-site café, for a red-bean latte. ✆ *8–11 Jeongdong • Map K5*

4 Former Russian Legation
Designed by Russian architect A.I. Sabatin, this is where King Gojong fled for protection after the assassination of his wife, Empress Myeongseong. ✆ *15–1 Jeongdong • Map J4*

5 Jungmyeonjeon 중명전
This structure, also designed by Sabatin, was used as a royal library by King Gojong. He signed the Eulsa Treaty here in 1905, paving the way for Japanese annexation. ✆ *1–11 Jeongdong • Map K5 • Open 10am–4pm Tue–Sun*

6 Bank of Korea Museum 한국은행 화폐금융박물관
This Japanese-designed structure now houses a museum showcasing rare notes and coins from around the world. ✆ *110 Namdaemunno 3-ga • Map L6 • 759 4881 • 10am–5pm Tue–Sun*

7 Seoul City Hall 서울특별시 청사
Currently being partially reconstructed, City Hall was first built by the Japanese in 1926 and housed the offices of the city's local government after liberation in 1945. ✆ *31 Taepyungno 1-ga • Map L5*

8 Myeongdong 도가훈
This shopping area probably receives more visitors than Insadong. The majority come here to buy branded clothing, handbags, or make-up. ✆ *Map M6*

9 Myeongdong Cathedral 라크레
The focus of Korea's burgeoning Catholic faith, this cathedral, dating from 1892, is the oldest parish church in the land. ✆ *2-ga 1 Myeongdong • Map N5 • 774 1784*

10 Deoksugunggil 서울에서 둘째로 잘하는 집
Deoksugunggil is one of Seoul's most charming roads. However, it was once home to the city's divorce courts, and locals believe that couples walking here will soon break up. ✆ *Map K5*

Price Categories

For the equivalent of a meal for two made up of a range of dishes, or one large dish, with half a bottle of wine.

W	under W10,000
WW	W10,000–20,000
WWW	W20,000–50,000
WWWW	W50,000–100,000
WWWWW	over W100,000

Stylish interior of Pierre Gagnaire à Séoul

10 Places to Eat

1 Woo Lae Oak 우래옥
Seoul's most famous restaurant for *naengmyeon* – buckwheat noodles in a cold soup (*mul naengmyun*) or sauce (*bibim naengmyun*). ✆ 118–1 Jogyodong • Map D2 • 2265 0151 • WW

2 The Korea House
한국의 집
Indulge in a huge banquet similar to those once eaten by the Joseon royalty. ✆ 80–2 Pildong • Map F6 • 2266 9101 • WWWWW

3 Pierre Gagnaire à Séoul
피어레 강나루 어 서울
A swanky restaurant serving scrumptious French haute cuisine – magnificent dishes made with Korean ingredients. ✆ 1 Sogongdong • Map L5 • 317 7181 • WWWWW

4 Samarkand 누룩
This simple Uzbek restaurant is frequented by the traders from Seoul's little "Russia Town." ✆ 162 Gwanghuidong • Map D2 • 2277 261 • WW

5 Congdu Iyagi 콩두 이야기
Superbly prepared "neo-Korean" dishes are served at this small restaurant. ✆ 2–1 Sinmunno • Map K4 • 722 7002 • WWWWW

6 Gwangjang Market
돌담길
There are two intersecting lanes of snack stands and eateries in this popular market. Ask the locals for suggestions. ✆ Map D2 • WW

7 31 Sky Lounge
31 스카이라운지
Once a hangout for VIPs and the military elite, this place is now charmingly retro in appearance, and the buffet spreads are both varied and delicious. ✆ 10–2 Gwancheoldong • Map M4 • 739 4619 • WW

8 Sushi Cho 스시 조
This restaurant is located in the Westin Chosun hotel (*see p114*), and the sushi served here is acclaimed even by the hotel's Japanese visitors. ✆ 87 Sogongdong • Map L5 • 317 0373 • WWWWW

9 Bulgogi Brothers
불고기 브라더스
A great place for barbecued meat, this place is popular with locals and visitors alike. ✆ 84 Seoul Finance Center • Map M5 • 775 7871 • WWW

10 Myeongdong Gyoja
명동교자
Delicious dumplings at bargain prices – it's little wonder that the place is jam-packed every day at lunchtime. ✆ 25–2 Myeongdong • Map M6 • 776 5348 • W

Left **Gwangjang Market** Center **Lotte Department Store** Right **Codes Combine**

TOP 10 Places to Shop

1 Shinsegae Department Store 신세계 백화점
The oldest department store in Korea is still one of its best. Clothing from most of Korea's famous designers is on display in the luxury wing, and there are great cafés on site (see p77).

2 Dongdaemun Market 동대문 시장
This is a huge market area with high-rise towers, malls, covered arcades and outdoor shacks, though most shoppers come here for cheap clothing and handbags (see p16).

3 Euljiro Underground Shopping Arcade
을지로 지하 쇼핑 아케이드
One of the world's longest shopping arcades, Euljiro is pleasingly retro – particularly the clothing favored by older Koreans. ❊ 161 Euljiro 2-ga • Map M5

4 Gwangjang Market 광장 시장
Most come here for the food, though it's also famous for silk and other fabrics. There's a great used-clothing market on the second floor on the western flank (see p16).

5 Lotte Department Store 롯데 백화점
A huge department store with an array of Korean clothing labels. The basement has Western food-stuffs. ❊ 1 Sogongdong • Map H5 • 771 2500 • Open 10:30am–8pm daily

6 Åland 올란드
The ground floor has clothing and footwear, and a range of used and vintage clothing on the top level. In between there's a range of funky stationery. ❊ 53–6 Myeongdong • Map M6 • 318 7640 • Open 9am–10pm daily

7 Codes Combine 코데스콤바인
This local unisex label has edgy designs. There are several stores across the city, including in the Coex and Times Square malls, and one in Myeongdong. ❊ 22–1 Chungmuro • Map M6 • 776 6385 • Open 10am–10pm daily

8 Namdaemun Market 남대문 시장
A fascinating place with hundreds of stores and stalls selling inexpensive clothing and footwear. ❊ 49 Namchangdong • Map C3 • Open noon–5pm daily

9 Donghwa Duty Free 동화면세점
This store has a huge range of alchoholic drinks and cosmetics – just bring along your flight ticket to reap the tax benefits. ❊ 211 Sejongno • Map L3 • 399 3000 • Open 9:30am–8:30pm daily

10 Monocollection 모노콜렉션
This popular fabric brand has stores at the airport, at The Plaza hotel (see p114), and has some wares in the Yido Pottery shop (see p72). ❊ City Hall • Map L5 • 310 7539 • Open 9am–9pm daily

Left **Baekseju Maeul** Right **Coffee Bean & Tea Leaf**

🔟 Bars & Cafés

1 Baekseju Maeul
백세주마을
This restaurant specializes in a "draught" version of Baekseju. It also sells *ihwaju* – a stronger, thicker version of *makgeolli*. ⊗ *256 Gwancheoldong • Map M4 • 720 0055*

2 Pierre's Bar 피어레스 바
A glitzy bar adjoining the Pierre Gagnaire à Séoul restaurant (see p79). Try the after-work special set – one of Pierre's signature cocktails, with a few delectable cakes from the kitchen. ⊗ *35 F Lotte Hotel, 1 Sogongdong • Map M5 • 317 7181*

3 Naos Nova 나오스 노바
Cool bar with a great wine list, a superb range of whiskies, plus some excellent *sake*. ⊗ *448–120 Huamdong • Map C3 • 754 2202*

4 Nu-Look 누룩
A dedicated *makgeolli* bar. You'll have to buy food to accompany your drink. ⊗ *38–1 Myeongdong • Map M5 • 772 9555*

5 Coffee Bean & Tea Leaf
커피빈 앤 티리프
One branch of this chain, on the Seoul Finance Center's second basement level, boasts a Victoria Arduino Venus Century espresso machine, of which only 100 were ever made. ⊗ *84 Taepyeongno • Map L4 • 753 2374*

6 Doldamgil 돌담길
Small café set into the grounds of Deoksugung palace (see p75). ⊗ *5–1 Jeongdong • Map K5*

7 Goyangi Darakbang
고양이 다락방
You can pet a cat here, while drinking your *macchiato*. ⊗ *51–14 Myeongdong • Map M5 • 318 3123*

8 Lounge Bar 153
라운지 바 153
A stylish bar with a good range of cocktails and wines. There is live jazz on Friday evenings. ⊗ *1–153 Sinmunno • Map K4 • 3210 3351*

9 Leonidas 레오니다스
Besides authentic Belgian chocolates, Leonidas offers a range of coffees. ⊗ *2–1 Myeongdong • Map M5 • 318 1312*

10 Gildeulyeojigi 길들에오지기
A café-cum-restaurant with the usual coffee options, as well as a few distinctly Korean choices – try the red-bean latte. ⊗ *8–11 Jeongdong • Map K5 • 319 7083*

Left **Café, Leeum art museum** Center **Aircraft, War Memorial of Korea** Right **Dragon Hill Spa**

Yongsan and Around

YONGSAN IS BY FAR THE MOST COSMOPOLITAN DISTRICT *in Seoul, boasting a truly global array of restaurants and some of the trendiest bars and clubs in the city. Not so long ago, however, its very name had negative connotations – an American military base was established here during the Korean War, and the bars and brothels were frequented by stressed-out soldiers. Nowadays the military presence is dwindling, the brothels have all but disappeared, and the area has some interesting sights on offer, such as the War Memorial, which lies adjacent to the American military base, the Leeum Art Museum, and Korea's National Museum.*

Main Hall, National Museum

View from Namsan

🔟 Sights

1. National Museum of Korea
2. Namsan
3. Leeum, Samsung Museum of Art
4. Bespoke Tailoring
5. War Memorial of Korea
6. Haebangchon and Gyeongnidan
7. Dragon Hill Spa
8. Antiques Alley
9. Homo Hill
10. Blue Square

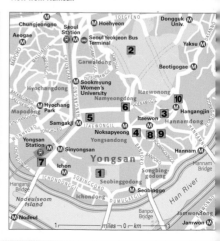

Interior of the National Museum of Korea

1 National Museum of Korea 국립중앙박물관

Korea was under the control of several kings from 57 BC to 1910, and relics from 2,000 years of dynastic rule are on display in this gigantic museum. Along with the treasures within, the parklike grounds boast various trails centered on a beautiful lake. Located on the other side of the museum is Yongsan Garrison, an American military base *(see pp14–15)*.

2 Namsan 남산

Rising up to the north of Yongsan is Namsan, a small mountain with various sights which can easily take half a day to explore. On the Yongsan side, the main attractions are a series of mazelike pathways that meander through the woods past small lakes and viewing platforms *(see pp18–19)*.

3 Leeum, Samsung Museum of Art 리움, 삼성미술관

The Leeum, as it is almost universally known, is one of the most esteemed museums in the country. Three acclaimed architects – Rem Koolhaas, Mario Botta, and Jean Nouvel – were roped in for the project, and the result is a beautiful symphony of architectural styles. The museum is split into several halls, each with a distinctive and original design. Unfortunately, tickets are often valid only for a specific window of time, and there are extremely strict restrictions on photography – check the website for more information. ◈ *747–18 Hannamdong • Map D4 • 2014 6901 • Open 10:30am–6pm Tue–Sun • Adm • leeum.samsungfoundation.org*

Tailored clothing

4 Bespoke Tailoring

Itaewon, a smaller district within Yongsan, has long been home to an array of tailors, the majority of whom specialize in making suits and shirts. Compared to international standards, prices here are very low, and though quality varies it can be very high indeed. Hamilton Shirts and Hahn's Custom Tailoring have an excellent reputation. ◈ *Hamilton Shirts: Hamilton Shirts 58–5 Itaewondong; Map R5 • Hahn's Custom Tailoring: 34–16 Itaewondong; Map R5*

Homosexuality in Korea

Although homosexuality is still often regarded as a "foreign disease" in Korean society, there are signs that the prejudice is slowly decreasing. The best evidence of this is the increasing number of locals – gay and straight alike – visiting the bars of Itaewon's "Homo Hill." Korea's first openly gay celebrity, Hong Seok-cheon, opened a small restaurant here after he came out in 2000 – paving the way for the rest of the gay population in Seoul.

War Memorial of Korea
전쟁기념관

Major wars have punctuated Korean history – the civil war in the early 1950s created North Korea and South Korea, two nations that are still in a state of conflict to this day. Though warfare may seem a rather morbid subject for a museum, the exhibitions in this large complex are quite absorbing; information on the Korean War is relayed with care, and the main building is surrounded by a whole regiment's worth of planes, rocket launchers, and similar artifacts. ◈ 8 Yongsandong 1-ga • Map C4 • 709 3139 • Open 9am–6pm Tue–Sun • www.warmemo.or.kr

6 Haebangchon and Gyeongnidan
해방촌, 경리단

Located to the west of central Itaewon, Haebangchon and Gyeongnidan are two adjoining areas home to many of Seoul's expatriates. Unlike high-rise, high-energy Itaewon, they are essentially typical Seoul neighborhoods with a relaxed, cosmopolitan twist – new bars and restaurants seem to open on a weekly basis. ◈ Map Q5

Dragon Hill Spa

7 Dragon Hill Spa
드래곤 힐 스파

The largest and most famous spa in Seoul, this is a delight to visit. Across its six levels, you'll find dozens of pools ranging from freezing cold to boiling hot – some are infused with green tea, ginseng, and other herbs. There are also various steam rooms, including some lined with amethyst and

War Memorial of Korea

Most of the sights in this area lie on subway line 6.

others with traditional Korean mud walls. Should you so desire, you can even take a nap here – there are dark rooms with small sleeping berths, while on-site restaurants and snack bars ensure that you won't go hungry. ⓢ 40–713 Hangangno 3-ga • Map C4 • 797 0002 • Adm

8 Antiques Alley 골동품 골목

To the south of Itaewon subway station is a road lined with shops selling antiques, ranging from the small and intimate to vast repositories. Highlights among the area's offerings include furniture from the Joseon dynasty, which are beautifully simple in design. ⓢ Map R6

9 Homo Hill 호모 힐

A steep side-street running parallel to the main Itaewon street has achieved particular fame in Seoul. This is "Homo Hill," one of Korea's openly gay areas, and, as such, a trendsetter for Korean gay society as a whole. ⓢ Map S6

Performance in Blue Square

10 Blue Square 블루 스퀘어

With eight large floors, Blue Square is one of Korea's largest performance venues. Although the focus is on Korean-language musicals, it also hosts occasional concerts. ⓢ 727–56 Hannamdong • Map S4 • 1544 1591 • Adm

A Day in Yongsan

Morning

🕐 Begin the day by visiting the grand **National Museum of Korea**, which is home to thousands of artifacts from Korea's long dynastic history. Two thousand years of regal rule ended with the Japanese occupation, which was almost immediately followed by the catastrophic Korean War in the 1950s. Relics from this conflict are on display in the **War Memorial of Korea**, just a short taxi-ride from the National Museum. Also a short taxi-ride away is **Haebangchon**, a trendy district with excellent cafés, which are a boon to those who have spent all morning soaking up history. Try the coffee and cake at **Indigo** (see p89), before strolling on up to Itaewon proper for an early lunch at **OKitchen** (see p89).

Afternoon

After lunch, it's time for some shopping. Itaewon has a splendid range of low-cost tailors, with suits and shirts being their speciality. Those interested in home furnishings can head to **Antiques Alley**. In the evening, head to one of the area's popular restaurants for dinner – choose from a Brazilian barbeque at **Copacabana**, Italian fare at **La Bocca**, or authentic curries at **Wang Thai** (see p89). If you have any energy left, hit the bars and clubs – **District** is the new it-spot, while **Bungalow** (see p88), with its weird seating areas, is one of the quirkiest bars in Seoul.

Left **Glasses on display at Craftworks Taphouse** Right **JJ Mahoney's**

Bars & Clubs

1 Damotori
다모토리

Sample over 30 varieties of *makgeolli (see p44)* in this popular bar. It is mandatory to buy a small meal to go with the drink. ✆ 44–18 Yongsandong • Map Q4 • 8950 8362

2 District 디스트릭트
With three happening venues – Prost, Glam, and Club Mute – in one large classy complex, District is Itaewon's newest it-spot. ✆ 116–1 Itaewondong • Map R5 • 792 6164

3 Bungalow 방갈로
A long-running favorite, this bar features quirky seating areas: drink cocktails on a swing, down beers beside an outdoor pool, or sip wine sitting on a rug.
✆ 112–3 Itaewondong • Map R5 • 793 2344

4 Craftworks Taphouse
크래프트웍스 탭하우스
Very popular with local expats, this pub serves a variety of microbrewed beers and excellent grilled food.
✆ 651 Itaewondong • Map Q5 • 794 2537

5 All That Jazz
올댓재즈
This jazz bar opened in 1976 and has hosted most, if not all, Korean jazz artistes of note. ✆ 112–4 Itaewondong • Map R5 • 795 5701

6 Noxa 녹사
Restaurant by day and bar by night, Noxa is a stylish venue serving food till late evening.
✆ 671 Itaewondong • Map Q5 • 790 0776

7 Gecko's Terrace
객코스 가든
One of Itaewon's older bars, Gecko's Terrace exudes the earthy feel of Itaewon's past – pool, darts, raucous conversations, and cheap draught beer. ✆ 128–5 Itaewondong • Map R5 • 749 9425

8 Club Rococo
클럽 로코코
Located in the basement of the IP Boutique hotel *(see p115)*, this hip club has attracted top international DJs and is packed on weekends. ✆ 732–32 Hannamdong • Map S5 • 790 2269

9 Ruf XXX
루프 XXX
Close to the Grand Hyatt *(see p114)*, this lounge bar is a wonderful place to relax. Outdoor seating is available in warm weather. ✆ 5–27 Itaewondong • Map R5 • 511 2570

10 JJ Mahoney's
JJ 마호니스
A lively bar located in the Grand Hyatt, JJ Mahoney's has a dance floor and a poolside terrace with a terrific view of southern Seoul. ✆ 322 Sowollo • Map S5 • 799 8601

Price Categories

For the equivalent of a meal for two made up of a range of dishes, or one large dish, with half a bottle of wine.

W	under W10,000
WW	W10,000–20,000
WWW	W20,000–50,000
WWWW	W50,000–100,000
WWWWW	over W100,000

Left **Passion 5 bakery** Right **Exterior of OKitchen**

🔟 Places to Eat

1 OKitchen 오키친
Housed in a converted *hanok* abode, OKitchen offers an interesting mix of Korean, Japanese, and European styles. ❧ 168–14 Itaewondong • Map R6 • 797 6420 • WWW

2 Copacabana 코파카바나
Itaewon now has several *churrascarias* (Brazilian-style steakhouses), but Copacabana was the first, and it remains the best. ❧ 119–9 Itaewondong • Map R6 • 796 1660 • WWW

3 Sihwadam 시화담
A favorite with dignitaries and businessmen, this pricey restaurant serves superb food. The courses are gigantic. ❧ 5–5 Itaewondong • Map R4 • 798 3311 • WWWWW

4 Passion 5 패션 5
Indulge in the excellent ice cream and chocolate served in this bakery, the headquarters of the Paris Baguette chain. ❧ 729–64 Hannamdong • Map S5 • 2071 9505 • WW

5 Indigo 인디고
Located in the fascinating neighborhood of Haebangchon (*see p86*), this popular café serves delicious sandwiches, cakes, and brunch. ❧ 46 Yongsandong • Map Q4 • 749 0508 • W

6 Vatos Tacos 바코스 타코스
Enjoy the Korean-style tacos and chili fries in this eatery. ❧ 2nd Floor, 181–8 Itaewondong • Map R6 • 797 8226 • WW

7 La Bocca 라 보카
The pastas and desserts in this Italian restaurant are simply fantastic. ❧ 737–37 Hannamdong • Map S5 • 790 5907 • WWW

8 Wang Thai 왕 타이
Don't be fooled by the low-key entrance – both locals and expatriates swear by this modest Thai restaurant. ❧ 176–2 Itaewondong • Map Q6 • 749 2746 • WW

9 N Grill 엔 그릴
Head to this revolving restaurant in N Seoul Tower for splendid 360-degree views of Seoul. ❧ N Seoul Tower • Map D3 • 3455 9297 • WWWWW

10 Petra 페트라
A Jordanian restaurant, Petra has a great range of dips and grilled meats. ❧ 552 Itaewondong • Map R5 • 790 4433 • WW

Around Town – Yongsan and Around

Share your travel recommendations on **traveldk.com**

89

Left **Landscaped grounds at Ewha Womans University** Right **Exterior of Sangsangmadang**

Western Seoul

THOUGH A LITTLE LIGHT ON ACTUAL TOURIST SIGHTS, *the western chunk of Central Seoul offers an interesting introduction to contemporary Korean culture. Of particular note is the university belt north of the Hangang river – more than 100,000 Seoulites study in these prestigious and artistically inclined universities. Upon graduating, many students find work in Yeouido, the most important financial district in Korea and home to its National Assembly, the largest church in the world, and a fascinating fish market.*

Shoppers at Sangsangmadang

63 City

🔟 Sights

1. The Universities
2. Jeoldusan Martyrs' Shrine
3. Luxury Su
4. Sangsangmadang
5. Nightlife
6. Coffee Culture
7. Noryangjin Fisheries Wholesale Market
8. 63 City
9. Seonyudo
10. Yoida Full Gospel Church

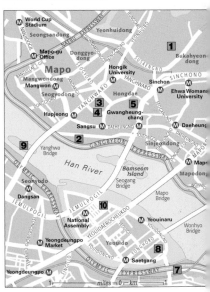

Ewha Womans University

The Universities

The universities of Western Seoul are interesting sights in their own right. Although park-like in nature, there's a sense of history around, too. Yonsei University was established in 1885 and Ewha Womans University the following year, and some of the main buildings in these two sites have survived the tumultuous years of dynastic rule and Western-style experimentation. ❧ *Yonsei University: 50 Yonseiro; Map B2; 1599 1885 • Ewha Womans University: 11–1 Daehyeondong; Map B2; 3277 2114*

Jeoldusan Martyrs' Shrine 절두산

Though Christianity is now Korea's main religion, Christians were once actively persecuted in the country. Nine French missionaries were executed in 1866, which prompted a purge of local Catholic converts. Many were beheaded on the small cliff of Jeoldusan, on which a shrine has now been built in memorial. Mother Teresa and Pope John Paul II visited the shrine in the 1980s to pay their respects. ❧ *96–1 Hapjeongdong • Map A3 • 312 4434*

Luxury Su 럭셔리 수

Karaoke bars are even more popular in Korea than in their homeland of Japan – rare is the road that doesn't have at least one *noraebang* (singing room). Given their ubiquitous nature, few *noraebang* have achieved particular fame, but Luxury Su is a major exception to the rule. Rooms here have been artistically decorated, and those at the front of the building have huge windows, making a rather public display of their patrons' singing. ❧ *367–39 Seogyodong • Map Q2*

Sangsangmadang 상상마당

Rising up next door to Luxury Su is the stylish Sangsangmadang building complex. Within it, there is a gallery and an art cinema, with installations at the former often governed by what's showing at the latter. There's also a café on the top floor, and a ground-floor shop sells trinkets made by students from the local university. ❧ *367–5 Seogyodong • Map Q2 • 330 6200 • Art market & gallery: Open 1–10pm daily; Cinema: Open 12:30–8pm daily*

Sculpture at the Jeoldusan Martyrs' Shrine

University Life

Most Koreans attend institutes of higher education, and competition for university seats in Seoul is quite intense. As a result, many children attend academies from the age of 5, their evenings and weekends monopolized by study.

However, once they're at a university, they let their hair down – almost every university is surrounded by bars, restaurants, karaoke rooms, and love motels.

Nightlife

The Hongdae area in Western Seoul has long been Seoul's style lab, particularly in terms of nightlife. This was where Korea's first Western-style clubs opened up, while subsequent trends have seen live-music venues, hookah lounges, and microbars open in the area. Hongdae has also been at the forefront of the recent *makgeolli* revolution – head to trendy Wolhyang or Dduk Tak *(see p94)* to try some.

Neon lights in Hongdae

Coffee Culture

Korean coffee culture took off in Western Seoul's university district – Starbucks opened its first Korean branch near Ewha Womans University in 1999. Though café chains still proliferate, there are plenty of independent cafés in the university area, most pertinently Café aA and Coffee Lab *(see p95)*, both located just outside Hongdae.

Coffee Lab

Noryangjin Fisheries Wholesale Market
노량진수산시장

Seoul's largest fish market has not yet found the kind of international fame Tsukiji in Tokyo did, though there's very little difference between the two. The hectic fish auctions make early morning the most interesting time to visit. In the evening, try some of the excellent seafood available in the restaurants located here *(see p95)*.

63 City 63시티

Seoul's most famous skyscraper, 63 City was built in 1985 on the island of Yeouido. Standing at a height of 820 ft (250 m), it was, on completion, the tallest building outside North America – hard to believe, given the new heights reached by skyscrapers built more recently in Dubai, Hong Kong, Shanghai, and countless other cities. Apart from the viewing platform, which is also an art gallery of sorts, there's the superb 63 World aquarium in the basement levels

The university area is served by subway line 2, and Yeouido by lines 5 and 9.

of the complex. ◈ *60 Yeouidodong
• Map B4 • 789 5663 • Open 10am–
10pm daily • Adm*

9 Seonyudo 선유도

This small, park-like islet,
located in the Hangang river,
makes it possible for visitors to
have a Seoul getaway without
having to leave the city at all. For
decades, Seonyudo was home to
the city's main water-treatment
plant. Now, however, substantial
gentrification has taken place,
and visitors are far more likely to
notice plants of a greener kind,
some of which have grown over
the old machinery. ◈ *Map A3*

Exterior, Yoido Full Gospel Church

10 Yoido Full Gospel Church
여의도 순복음 교회

Yeouido boasts one record – the
world's largest church. Though
the structure itself is smaller
than other churches around the
world, Yeouido's Full Gospel
Church has a membership of
over 100,000. There are seven
Sunday services held here, and
each is translated into over a
dozen languages. Regardless
of your religious sentiments,
visiting is an unusual and
interesting experience. ◈ *11
Yeouidodong • Map A4 • 782 4851
• www.english.fgtv.com*

A Day in Western Seoul

Morning

🕐 Those able to haul
themselves out of bed
before dawn breaks should
head over to **Noryangjin
Fisheries Wholesale
Market** to see its
fascinating daily fish
auction. If you aren't an
early riser, start your day
at Yeouido with coffee
and a pastry before
catching the view from
the top of the **63 City**
building. Then drop by
the excellent aquarium
in the basement. If it's
a Sunday, get yourself
over to the **Yoida Full
Gospel Church** – with
over 100,000 members,
it is the largest church
in the world.

Afternoon

The mazy pathways
of **Seonyudo** island are
ideal for a long afternoon
walk. You can also visit
the riverside **Jeoldusan
Martyrs' Shrine**. After
experiencing the peace
and quiet of these two
places, liven up your
evening by visiting
Hongdae, Korea's most
entertaining nightlife zone.
Try some street snacks
(see p95) and head to one
of the many bars in the
area. **Club Evans** and
Drug *(see p94)* are
excellent for live music,
but if you want a quieter
space, **BricX** *(see p94)* is a
basement bar with a great
loungey vibe – try one of
their delightful cocktails.
For interesting and fun
versions of *makgeolli*, the
local rice-wine popular
with visitors to the city,
stop by **Wolhyang** or
Dduk Ttak *(see p94)*. You
can also grab a cocktail-to-
go from **Vinyl** *(see p94)*.

Around Town – Western Town

Left **Takeaway cocktails at Vinyl** Center **Dduk Tak** Right **BricX**

Bars and Clubs

1 Wolhyang 울향
A trendy *makgeolli* bar, Wolhyang prides itself on a version made with "unwashed" brown rice. 🅂 *335–5 Seogyodong • Map S1 • 332 9202*

2 BricX 브릭 X
Enjoy the excellent cocktails made by the bartenders in this relaxed basement bar with a range of comfy seats, booths, and floor cushions. 🅂 *409–1 Seogyodong • Map Q3 • 795 5572*

3 Drug 드럭
One of the catalysts behind the Seoul indie music scene during the 1990s, Drug is a great bar to hang out in. Gigs take place roughly once a week. 🅂 *395–17 Seogyodong • Map Q2 • 322 3792*

4 Vinyl 비닐
This small bar serves cocktails in vinyl pouches. There are only a couple of tables here, so most customers take their drinks away with them. 🅂 *411–1 Seogyodong • Map R3 • 322 4161*

5 Dduk Tak 뚝딱
A great example of a "fun" *makgeolli* bar. With flavors like banana, kiwi, honey, and even tomato on offer, the *makgeolli* here is not exactly Korean, but tasty nonetheless. 🅂 *330–17 Seogyodong • Map A3 • 336 6883*

6 Ggot 쥐갓
Slightly difficult to locate, Ggot is a great basement bar worth the search. Its understated vibe changes on weekends when it becomes a live-music venue. 🅂 *325–1 Seogyodong • Map S1 • 324 4757*

7 Ho Bar 호 바
This chain of bars is a phenomenon – at the last count, there were more than 10 in the Hongdae area. Ho Bar 3, located downhill from the Hongik university entrance, is usually the busiest. 🅂 *Ho Bar 3: B1 358–1 Seogyodong • Map A3 • 336 6011*

8 Club Evans 클럽 에반스
One of Korea's most respected jazz bars, Club Evans hosts two sets each night, with the more accomplished ensembles usually saved for weekends. 🅂 *407–3 Seogyodong • Map R3 • 337 8361*

9 NB 엔비
A gigantic hip-hop club, NB has DJs playing the latest hits. It is best to get here early to avoid the queue. 🅂 *362–4 Seogyodong • Map R2 • 326 1716*

10 Mansion 맨션
A trendy lounge bar on weekdays, Mansion is very popular with students on weekend nights. 🅂 *368–22 Seogyodong • Map Q2 • 3143 4037*

Café aA

Price Categories

For the equivalent of a meal for two made up of a range of dishes, or one large dish, with half a bottle of wine.

W	under W10,000
WW	W10,000–20,000
WWW	W20,000–50,000
WWWW	W50,000–100,000
WWWWW	over W100,000

🔟 Places to Eat

1 Noryangjin Fisheries Wholesale Market
노량진수산시장

Seoul's fish market has a few restaurants where you can order from the menu, or bring your purchases from the market to be cooked. 🔊 *13–8 Noryangjindong* • *Map B5* • *814 2211* • *WWW*

2 Oyori 오요리
This restaurant serves a range of international food. Staffed by single immigrant mothers, Oyori's profits go, in part, toward schooling their children. 🔊 *409–10 Seogyodong* • *Map Q3* • *332 5525* • *WW*

3 Bukchon Sonmandu
북촌손만두

A shack which serves a range of cheap dumplings. Its picture menus make ordering a simple affair. 🔊 *332–1 Seogyodong* • *Map R1* • *333 1282* • *W*

4 Saemaeul Sikdang
새마을식당

The main Hongdae outlet of this barbecued-meat restaurant chain offers high-quality meat at low prices. 🔊 *331–18 Seogyodong* • *Map A3* • *332 0120* • *WW*

5 Pakito's 파키토스
One of the best Spanish restaurants in Seoul, Pakito's serves superb paella. 🔊 *330–46 Seogyodong* • *Map A3* • *6407 6064* • *WW*

6 678
Right in the middle of the main nightlife district, this barbecued-meat restaurant is a popular pre- or post-drinks venue. 🔊 *408–22 Seogyodong* • *Map A3* • *326 0678* • *WW*

7 Ryugyeongok
류경옥

This unpretentious restaurant serves excellent *naengmyeon* – a cold yet spicy North Korean dish made with buckwheat noodles (*see p43*). It also serves beer and berry wine from north of the border. 🔊 *426–15 Gongdeokdong* • *Map B3* • *711 0797* • *WW*

8 Street Food
The Hongdae area is packed with vendors serving cheap snacks to hungry students. The T-junction near Sangsu station has street vendors selling fried, battered, tempura-like snacks known as *twigim*. 🔊 *Map R2* • *W*

9 Café aA 카페 aA
This fascinating café has one of Korea's finest furniture collections. 🔊 *408–11 Seogyodong* • *Map Q3* • *3143 7312* • *W*

10 Coffee Lab
커피 랩

This serves excellent coffee using a variety of beans and roasting implements. 🔊 *327–19 Seogyodong* • *Map S1* • *3143 0908* • *W*

95

Left **Visitors at Samsung D'light** Right **Coex Mall**

Southern Seoul

FOR MUCH OF SEOUL'S TIME AS CAPITAL *of the Joseon kingdom (1392–1910), the whole city was located north of the river, concentrated in a tight area between the Bugaksan and Namsan mountains. The baby boom that followed the Korean War, and the economic boom after that, resulted in a rapid expansion of the city, and Seoul's southern half is now even more populous than its north. While there's a little less for visitors to see south of the Hangang, it is certainly worth crossing the river to have a look at an area which sometimes feels like a different city: richer, more modern, more fashionable, and a window into the Korea of the future.*

🔟 Sights

1. Garosugil
2. Samsung D'light
3. Coex Mall
4. Bongeunsa
5. Samneung Tombs
6. Banpo Bridge
7. Seoul Olympic Park
8. Lotte World
9. Seoul National Cemetery
10. Gwacheon

Lotte World

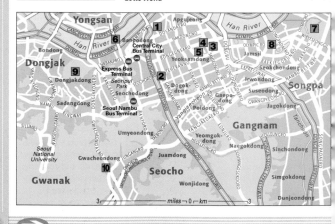

Coex Aquarium

Garosugil 가로수 길
1 Its name translates as "tree-lined road," and Garosugil is, indeed, lined with gingko trees. A once nondescript road, it has recently transformed into one of the trendiest parts of Seoul and has an ever-changing roster of cafés, boutiques, and restaurants. ◈ Map E4

Samsung D'light 삼성 디 라이트
2 Although Gangnam station is surrounded by neon-lit streets and has many restaurants, bars, and cafés, there is little of note to tourists in the area. The only exception is the headquarters of Samsung Electronics – the most important wing of Korea's world-famous corporation. A few of the lower floors have been converted into a fascinating showroom of past, present, and future Samsung gadgets, and feature plenty of interactive, hi-tech displays. ◈ Samsung Electronics Building, 1320–10 Seochodong • Map E6 • 2255 2262 • Open 10am–7pm Mon–Fri

Coex Mall 코엑스 몰
3 Seoul's main shopping mall, Coex is an entirely underground affair, and a highly popular rainy-day magnet for Seoulites. For those who'd like to do something other than shop, there is a gigantic aquarium (see p61) as well as the Pulmuone Kimchi Museum, which is the best place for visitors to learn how to make Korea's most famous dish. ◈ 159 Samseongdong; Map F5 • Aquarium: 6002 6200; Open 10am–8pm daily; Adm • Pulmuone Kimchi Museum: 6002 6546; Open 10am–6pm Tue–Sun; Adm • www.coex.co.kr/

Bongeunsa 봉은사
4 One of urban Seoul's few major Buddhist temples, Bongeunsa is even more attractive than Jogyesa, its north-of-the-river counterpart (see p10). When looking north from the entrance, visitors can see a steep hill dotted with colorful wooden structures; if they look the other way from the top, they will see nothing but high-rise buildings – the rather interesting contrast of traditional and modern Seoul. ◈ 73 Samseongdong • Map F5 • 511 6070 • Open 3–10pm daily

The 8th-century Bongeunsa Buddhist temple

Korean Burial Mounds

Since time immemorial, Koreans have buried their dead in grass-covered mounds of earth. The rapid urbanization of the country has made this an extremely expensive practice – prohibitively so in Seoul. The Samneung complex and the Seoul National Cemetery are striking examples of this tradition.

Seoul Olympic Park

5 Samneung Tombs
선릉의 무덤

The royals of dynastic Korea were buried with their possessions in large mounds of earth – a far simpler and more natural alternative to the pyramids of Egypt. The tombs in this calm, tree-filled park are the ones most accessible for visitors to Seoul – this was the burial site for two kings and one queen from the Joseon dynasty. The queen in question, Jeonghyeon (1462–1530), is said to have founded the nearby temple of Bongeunsa.
⊙ *135–4 Samseongdong • Map F5*
• Open Mar–Oct: 9am–6:30pm Tue–Sun, Nov–Feb: 9am–5:30pm Tue–Sun • Adm

6 Banpo Bridge 반포 대교
By day, Banpo Bridge is just one of two dozen bridges straddling the Hangang, the river that bisects Central Seoul. In the evening, however, each side of the bridge is lined with high-pressure water jets, which essentially make a centipede-shaped fountain of the entire structure. The display is illuminated with thousands of LEDs, making for one of Seoul's more memorable nighttime experiences. ⊙ *Map D5*

7 Seoul Olympic Park
서울 올림픽 공원

Seoul hosted the Summer Olympics in 1988 *(see p35)*, and venues from the games are still in use today. This park is one of the best places in Seoul for an afternoon stroll, and on weekends it often hosts community events. The Olympic Museum located in the park is also interesting.
⊙ *88 Bangidong • Map H4 • 410 1114*
• Olympic Park: Open 6am–10pm daily; Olympic Museum: Open 10am–6pm Tue–Sun

8 Lotte World 롯데 월드
The gigantic Lotte World complex is a real favorite with the young and young-at-heart alike. Most come for the theme park, which is split into indoor and outdoor sections – the indoor component weaves in and out of a large shopping mall, while the outdoor section is arranged

Fountain at Banpo Bridge

Southern Seoul is well served by the subway – lines 2 and 9 link many of its important destinations.

around an artificial lake.
There's also a folk museum
and an ice-skating rink.

🌐 40–1 Jamsildong • Map H5 • 411 2000
• Open 9:30am–10pm daily • Adm

9 Seoul National Cemetery
국립서울현충원

This cemetery is of major
historical importance. It is the
resting place of three former
presidents: Syngman Rhee,
the country's first leader; Park
Chung-hee, a dictatorial ruler,
yet the catalyst for Korea's
economic turnaround; and
Kim Dae-jung, winner of the
2000 Nobel Peace Prize.

🌐 San 44–7 Dongjakdong • Map C5
• 813 9625 • Open Mar–Oct: 6am–8pm
daily, Nov–Feb: 7am–5pm Sun–Fri

Seoul Grand Park, Gwacheon

10 Gwacheon 과천

A half-hour subway
ride from Central Seoul, the
neighboring city of Gwacheon
is markedly different in feel
from the capital. It boasts a
number of interesting sights,
including Seoul Grand Park,
the National Museum of
Contemporary Art, Gwacheon
National Science Museum, and
Seoul Race Park. Gwacheon is
also home to Seoul Land, the
widest swath of parkland in
Seoul, and there are a few hiking
trails in the nearby mountains
(see pp30–31).

A Day in Southern Seoul

Morning

🕐 Begin your day with
coffee at **The Lounge**
(see p100) – a snazzy
café atop the Park Hyatt.
You can also try one
of their signature
smoothies. After this,
the remainder of the
morning can be spent
soaking up a bit of
Korean culture. The
Buddhist temple of
Bongeunsa offers great
opportunities for
photographs, while the
Samneung Tombs – the
royal burial mounds
located next to Seolleung
subway station – are both
educational about local
history and perfect for a
morning walk.

Afternoon

It's over to trendy
Garosugil for lunch – try
some deliciously unhealthy
hoddeok (Korean pancakes)
with different toppings at
West 'n East *(see p100)*,
and wash them down with
a red-bean latte. Then it's
time to hit the area's
shops. There are plenty in
Garosugil, but label-
hunters should head over
to **Apgujeongno** (east of
Apgujeong subway station)
for the flagship stores of
major international labels.
The side-streets around
Dosan Park *(see p102)* are
known for their small but
quirky boutiques. If you
are tired after all the
shopping, make your way
to nearby **Goongyeon** *(see
p101)* where you can dine
like a Korean king. After
that, it'll be time to get
yourself over to **Banpo
Bridge** – straddling the
Hangang, this structure
turns into a gigantic,
spectacular fountain as
night approaches.

Left **Coffee Smith** Right **West 'n East** exterior

Cafés

Café Madang 카페 마당
An attractive, chic café located in the basement of the Hermès building in Apgujeong. ⊗ 630–26 Sinsadong • Map E4 • 3015 3208

74
With its bright, airy interior, 74 is highly popular from late morning to late evening. It serves a wide range of light meals and a good selection of teas and ice creams. ⊗ 83–20 Cheongdamdong • Map E4 • 542 7412

Hangang Bridge Cafés
Six bridges over the Hangang have small, quirky cafés at their southern ends. All offer great views of the river.

West 'n East 웨스트 엔 이스트
Serving a range of desserts and drinks, West 'n East fuses Western styles with Korean ingredients. Try a green tea or red-bean latte, or hoddeok pancakes with various fillings and toppings. ⊗ 518–8 Sinsadong • Map E4 • 3445 0919

The Lounge 더라운지
Located in the Park Hyatt hotel (see p114), this place offers superb views of Seoul and has excellent drinks and desserts. Try the patbingsu – a Korean sweet made with cream, ice shavings, and fruity toppings. ⊗ Map F5 • 2016 1205

Namu Geuneul 나무그늘
At Namu Geuneul, take your socks off and let tiny fish nibble dead skin from your feet while you enjoy a cup of coffee and a variety of snacks. ⊗ 1305–3 Seochodong • Map D6 • 6442 1260

Coffee Smith 커피 스미스
One of the larger cafés in Seoul, Coffee Smith is spread over two levels; three in summer, when tables and chairs spill onto the street. ⊗ 541–7 Sinsadong • Map E5 • 3446 9383

Miel 미엘
With a range of comfy seats arranged around honeycomb-like slats and hexagons, Miel has the appearance of a giant beehive. It serves excellent drinks. ⊗ 94–3 Cheongdamdong • Map E4 • 512 2395

Baek Eok Café 백억 카페
This large, trendy café's name is a nod to the affluence of the Gangnam area – "baek" is the Korean word for 100 and "eok" the term for 100 million. ⊗ 618–11 Yeoksamdong • Map F5 • 568 7788

10 Corso Como 10 골프 코스 코모
Seoul's branch of the Milanese designer label comes with its own chic café and, despite huge local competition, remains very popular. ⊗ 79 Cheongdamdong • Map E4 • 547 3010

Price Categories

For the equivalent of a meal for two made up of a range of dishes, or one large dish, with half a bottle of wine.

W	under W10,000
WW	W10,000–20,000
WWW	W20,000–50,000
WWWW	W50,000–100,000
WWWWW	over W100,000

Gorilla in the Kitchen

TOP 10 Places to Eat

1 Goongyeon 궁연
This excellent restaurant serves traditional banquet meals. Dishes vary by season. ⓈⓈ 125–23 Cheongdamdong • Map E4 • 3673 1104 • WWWWW

2 Crystal Jade Palace 크리스탈 자개 궁전
One of the city's top restaurants, the Crystal Jade Palace serves a mix of Cantonese and Shanghainese specialities. ⓈⓈ 159–8 Samseongdong • Map F5 • 3288 8101 • WWWWW

3 Jung Sikdang 정식당
The food in Jung Sikdang is a mélange of Korean and Western tastes. ⓈⓈ 649–7 Sinsadong • Map E5 • 517 4654 • WWWWW

4 Yu Ga Ne 유가네
A budget option, Yu Ga Ne serves inexpensive and delicious *dak-galbi*, a spicy chicken and lettuce dish, made in front of you on the table. ⓈⓈ 816–5 Yeoksamdong • Map F5 • 563 3392 • WWW

5 Tutto Bene 나무그늘
Superb pasta dishes served in a romantic setting – this Italian restaurant is a must-visit. ⓈⓈ 118–9 Cheongdamdong • Map E4 • 546 1489 • WWW

6 Oga No Kitchen 오가네
A Japanese restaurant offering a variety of fusion dishes and sakes. It has a lounge bar and terrace café. ⓈⓈ 645–8 Sinsadong • Map E5 • 514 0058 • WWWWW

7 Gorilla in the Kitchen 고릴라 인 키친
Complete with calculated calorie counts, this restaurant offers healthy dishes like salads, soups, and smoothies. ⓈⓈ 650 Sinsadong • Map E5 • 3442 1688 • WWW

8 Bamboo House 대나무 하우스
Specializing in barbecued meat, Bamboo House has multilingual staff, easy-to-read menus, and an excellent wine list. ⓈⓈ 658–10 Yeoksamdong • Map F5 • 566 0870 • WWWW

9 Suraon 수라온
This restaurant serves highly traditional meals. Apart from royal-style banquet courses, it also has an à la carte menu. ⓈⓈ 118–3 Banpodong • Map D5 • 595 0202 • WWWWW

10 Tang 탕
An attractive Vietnamese restaurant, Tang is most popular for its *salguksu* – a local version of Vietnam's famous pho noodle-soup. ⓈⓈ 601–1 Yeoksamdong • Map F5 • 554 0707 • WWW

Left **Window display, Boon the Shop** Center **Maison de Lee Young Hee** Right **Coex Mall**

TOP 10 Places to Shop

1 Boon the Shop 분 더 샵
A stylish luxury mall, this stocks top local brands and a smattering of international labels. The main foyer functions as an art exhibition space of sorts. *82–3 Cheongdamdong • Map E4 • 317 0397*

2 Galleria 갤러리아
Regarded as the most luxurious department store in Seoul, Galleria has a great selection of major labels. *515 Apgujeongdong • Map F4 • 3449 4114*

3 Maison de Lee Young Hee 이영희한복집
This boutique is owned by renowned Korean designer Lee Young Hee, who is known for creating contemporary and wearable styles of the *hanbok* – Korea's national dress. *665–5 Sinsadong • Map E5 • 547 0630*

4 Times Square 타임 스퀘어
A large mall, Times Square has most international high-street labels as well as a selection of local chains. *442 Yeongdeungpo-dong • Map A5 • 2638 2000*

5 Designer Stores 디자이너 스토어
A few designer stores in the Dosan Park area were designed by prominent architects – check out the space-age local flagship store of the Belgian label Ann Demeulemeester. *Map E5*

6 Dosan Park Boutiques 도산공원 뷰티크
If you are looking for local brands, poke around the small side-streets around Dosan Park to stumble upon its many charming boutiques. *649–9 Sinsadong • Map E5*

7 Daily Projects 매일 프로젝트
This small and funky shop has a great selection of brands from mostly up-and-coming local designers. They hold a flea market on Sundays. *1–24 Cheongdamdong • Map E4 • 3218 4072*

8 Garosugil 가로수길
Dotted with gingko trees, Garosugil has long been one of Seoul's most fashionable thoroughfares. *Map E4*

9 Coex Mall 코엑스 몰
In addition to an array of shops and restaurants, this underground mall also has the interesting Pulmuone Kimchi Museum to entertain visitors *(see p97)*. *159 Samseongdong • Map F5 • 6000 1162*

10 Homeplus Smart Virtual Store
홈 플러스 스마트 가상 스토어
Connected to the Seoullung subway station, this is a virtual store. Customers can register and buy goods with their cell phones after selecting them from flatscreen images arranged like two-dimensional goods racks.

Left **Interior of Timber House bar** Right **T-Lound**

ⓉⓄⓅ⑩ Bars and Clubs

1 Moon Jar 달 항아리
The best and most popular *makgeolli* bar south of the Hangang river, Moon Jar offers a country-wide selection of the milky rice-wine, as well as an excellent range of fruit juice-blended cocktails. ✆ *644–19 Sinsadong • Map E5 • 541 6118*

2 Rainbow 무지개
Leave your shoes at the door. Once inside this laid-back place, relax on the floor cushions while listening to groovy tunes and, perhaps, enjoying a hookah. ✆ *1308–11 Seochodong • Map D6 • 3481 1869*

3 Timber House 목재 하우스
Located in the Park Hyatt *(see p114)* this traditional bar offers a great selection of Japanese sake. ✆ *Map F6 • 2016 1234*

4 Club Eden 클럽 에덴
Colorful seats and illuminated drinks counters make this club, tucked under the Ritz-Carlton hotel, a favorite with Seoul's young crowd. ✆ *602 Yeoksamdong • Map F5 • 6447 0042*

5 Platoon Kunsthalle 플라톤 쿤스탄
This one-of-a-kind bar and restaurant, serving German beer and food, also doubles up as a gallery and performance space. ✆ *97–22 Nonhyeondong • Map E5 • 3447 1191*

6 Club Ellui 클럽 엘루이
This popular party spot can accommodate over 4,000 people. ✆ *129 Cheongdamdong • Map E4 • 9111 6205*

7 T-Lound 티 라운지
This sleek, four-level bar is at the top of Seoul's cocktail charts. Enjoy the delightful martinis and mojitos made by T-Lound's trained "mixologists." ✆ *83–13 Cheongdamdong • Map E4 • 517 7412*

8 Coffee Bar K 커피 바 K
This cozy bar has hundreds of varieties of whisky to choose from. ✆ *89–20 Cheongdamdong • Map E4 • 516 1970*

9 Club Answer 클럽 답변
Everyone wants to get onto the VIP level at this super exclusive club. ✆ *125–16 Cheongdamdong • Map E4 • 514 4311*

10 Club Mass 클럽 매스
The wild exterior lighting makes Club Mass hard to miss. ✆ *1306–8 Seochodong • Map D6 • 599 3165*

STREETSMART

SEOUL'S TOP 10

Left **Traditional *hanok*** Right **Fall colors at Changdeokgung palace**

TOP 10 Planning Your Trip

1 When to Go
Seoul is a year-round destination. Korean summers are hot, wet, and humid, though traveling in summer can still be enjoyable. Winter is long and cold, but the weather almost never affects transportation or opening hours, and snowfall is rare. However, spring (Apr–Jun) and fall (Sep–Oct) are by far the best times to visit.

2 What to Pack
South Korea is one of the most convenient places to travel – you could arrive with a few changes of clothing and be fine. Summer and winter temperatures will, however, govern your choice of clothing. Don't forget to bring wet-weather gear in the summer.

3 Weather
Temperatures in Seoul often soar over 86° F (30° C) in June and July, which are also by far the rainiest months of the year. The temperature rarely rises above 32° F (0° C) during December, January, and February, and can plummet below 5° F (-15° C), though there are blue skies most days. Spring (Apr–Jun) and fall (Sep–Oct) have clement weather and little rainfall.

4 Passports and Visas
Citizens of more than 100 nations, including the US, Canada, Australia, New Zealand, and most of Europe, are granted visa-free entry on arrival. The amount of time allowed in the country varies from one to six months – 90 days is most common, but check with your local South Korean embassy. Do remember to keep your passport with you at all times to serve as identification.

5 Insurance
It is unwise to travel without valid insurance – be sure to check the specifics of your policy, particularly whether or not it covers travel to South Korea. It is a good idea to obtain comprehensive travel insurance that covers health and personal belongings.

6 Customs
Travelers carrying more than US $10,000 in cash must declare the specific amount on arrival. Penalties for carrying drugs can be severe.

7 Where to Stay
The bulk of Seoul's best hotels are clustered around City Hall to the north of the river and Gangnam to the south; the former is more convenient for sightseeing. Myeongdong district, near City Hall, is well-located and has a profusion of motels and mid-range hotels, while the student district of Hongdae is best for both nightlife and youth hostels. The Bukchon area has a dozen wooden *hanok* guesthouses – the city's most traditional places to stay.

8 Maps
The profusion of maps available from Seoul's tourist information offices, together with the foolproof, dual-language route maps in all subway stations and trains, make Seoul an easy city to get around.

9 Electricity
Electrical current is 220 volts AC – the same as Europe, but double of that in North America. As in much of Europe, wall sockets in Seoul also take plugs with two round pins. British and Australian appliances, however, will need an adaptor, and North American ones may also need a transformer.

10 Time Zone
South Korea is 9 hours ahead of GMT, 14 hours ahead of US East Coast time, 17 hours ahead of US West Coast time, and an hour behind Sydney, Australia. Daylight savings times are not used.

Preceding pages **Souvenir shop in Insadong**

Left **Korean Air planes** Center **Commuters in the subway** Right **Walking in Bukchon**

TOP 10 Getting There and Around

1 By Air from North America

There are direct flights to Incheon International Airport *(see p40)* from Atlanta, Chicago, Dallas, Detroit, Honolulu, Los Angeles, New York City, San Francisco, Seattle, and Washington D.C. in the USA; and from Toronto and Vancouver in Canada.
🌐 *www.airport.kr/eng/*

2 By Air from Europe

Direct, nonstop flights link Incheon International Airport with all major European cities, often with European flag-carriers as well as one or both of Korea's own airlines, Korean Air and Asiana. It's usually cheaper to fly via the Middle East. 🌐 *www.koreanair.com; www.flyasiana.com*

3 By Air from Asia

Incheon International Airport is connected to most major Asian airports by direct flights. There are numerous flights linking South Korea with cities in China and Japan; there are several connections each day to major cities such as Tokyo, Beijing, and Shanghai.

4 By Ferry

There are ferries from Incheon, a city just west of Seoul, to a dozen ports on the east Chinese coast. Most services run two or three times per week. The closest port to Beijing is Tanggu, which is a taxi-ride from Tianjin city. There are ferries most days from Busan (three hours from Seoul by train) to Fukuoka and Shimonoseki in western Japan; Fukuoka and Busan are also linked at least four times daily by faster catamarans.

5 Overland

South Korea's only international land border is with North Korea, and this has been off-limits to travelers for decades.

6 Getting Around by Subway

Seoul's subway system is excellent, and there is English-language signage in trains and stations alike. Prices start at W1,150 per journey, and rarely rise above W2,000 – you'll save money as well as time by buying a ticket from the slightly confusing machines, with a T-Money card *(see p108)*. Note that there's a direct line to Seoul train station from Incheon International Airport.

7 Getting Around by Bus

Unless you're able to read Korean, the bus system is likely to prove tricky to use. Again, prices start at W1,150, and drop by W100 with use of a T-Money card. The exceptions are buses from the airport, which start at W10,000 and race all over Seoul. Buses to most destinations in the excursions chapter *(see pp62–3)* leave from the Express Bus Terminal, south of the river on subway lines 3, 7, and 9.

8 Getting Around by Taxi

You'll rarely be too far from a taxi in Seoul. The fixed starting rate is W2,400, and unless you're heading across the city you'll most likely receive change for W10,000. Prices rise by 20 per cent after midnight. Taxi drivers are almost uniformly trustworthy, and though few speak English most will be able to access an interpreter on their in-car phones, should difficulties arise.

9 Getting Around by Train

Trains to other South Korean cities leave from Seoul and Yongsan stations, both north of the river on subway lines 1 and 4.

10 Getting Around on Foot

While not exactly a pedestrian's paradise, Seoul is relatively straightforward to get around on foot. It is possible to stroll between most destinations in the Palace Quarter and Central Seoul chapters.

Left **T-Money sign** Right **Korean and international magazines for sale**

TOP 10 Useful Information

1 Tourist Booths

Convenient tourist information booths can be found at quite a few places around the city, including Insadong, Myeongdong, Gangnam, and Bukchon Hanok Village. There are also a few booths inside Incheon International Airport. Staff can almost always speak English, have useful maps and pamphlets to hand out, and can also give advice on accommodations.

2 Useful Websites

Check out the official websites of the Korea Tourism Organization and the Seoul Tourism Organization; both are excellent sources of travel information. There are also some helpful websites on food and pop culture.
⊛ www.visitkorea.or.kr; www.visitseoul.net; www.fatmanseoul.com; www.eatyourkimchi.com

3 Useful Numbers

Operators on the official tourist lines of Seoul City and the Korea Tourism Organization are usually able to deal with most queries pertaining to transportation or tourist sights. In case of miscommunication, most taxi drivers can call up an interpreter for free from their in-car phones.
⊛ Korea Tourism Organization: 1330; Seoul City: 120

4 T-Money Cards

Available from most convenience stores and reloadable at all subway stations, these cards make getting around Seoul quite easy. These prepaid cards cost W3,000, and can be used on all subway trains, buses, and taxis. They can also be used as a cash-free payment alternative at most convenience stores and some public telephones.

5 Toilets

Public toilets are ubiquitous in Seoul, and there is never a charge for their use. Note, however, that poor plumbing systems mean that there's a risk of blockage if you put tissue paper down the toilet.

6 Magazines

Time, *Newsweek*, and *The Economist* are available in major bookstores. Among the local English-language monthlies, *10 Magazine* and *Seoul Selection* are recommended – some convenience stores stock them, and you may find copies at your hotel too.

7 Newspapers

The two main English-language dailies are *The Korea Times* and *The Korea Herald*. Both are found at newsstands across the city. The main American dailies are available in some of the higher-end hotels.

8 Language

Most young Seoulites can speak at least a little English, and almost all hotels and hostels have English-speaking staff. However, do not expect bus drivers, taxi drivers, and restaurant staff to speak in English. Still, it is quite easy to find restaurants and cafés with English-language menus in Central Seoul.

9 Tours and Tickets

Hourly tour buses run daily between the main sights from 9am to 6pm, and there are night bus tours at 8pm. There are also 2–3-hour-long walking tours of the Palace Quarter. Seoul City's tourist site has information on all these tours. The Integrated Palace Ticket for W10,000 includes admission to Jongmyo, Deoksugung, Changgyeonggung, Changdeokgung, and Gyeongbokung, and lasts up to a month. ⊛ www.visitseoul.net

10 Gay and Lesbian Seoul

Homosexuality was seen as a "foreign disease" by most Koreans until fairly recently. A certain stigma still persists, but most young Seoulites are now curious, rather than baffled, about the concept. The main foreigner-friendly gay areas are Itaewon for men, and Sinchon for women.

Left **Rush hour** Center **Motorcyclist on a sidewalk** Right **Buying tickets at the subway**

TOP 10 Things to Avoid

1 Rush Hour
In the hour leading up to 9am, buses and subway trains get very busy and clammy, and crowded stations during rush hour may be hard to avoid. Evenings are less of a problem as so many Seoulites are obliged to work overtime, but buses and taxis often get snarled up in traffic between 5 and 7pm.

2 Sidewalk Traffic
Seoul's sidewalks are often used by road traffic, primarily parked cars and delivery scooters. The police rarely take action in such circumstances, so keep your wits about you when walking around. Also note that some smaller streets have no pedestrian areas at all.

3 Blocked Toilets
Other than in high-end hotels, you will inevitably see waste-baskets next to toilets in Korea. Because of poor plumbing systems, toilets may block when a certain amount of used tissue is put down them. Be sure to use the waste baskets – being identified as the guilty party in a guesthouse or restaurant would be no fun at all.

4 Buying Tickets
If you're staying in Seoul for any longer than a couple of days, it is sensible to invest in T-Money, a prepaid transportation card. Bus drivers will accept coins and small notes, but you will hold up the line. Also, the ticket machines in subway stations take a little figuring out if you haven't used one before – even the locals get confused from time to time.

5 Midnight Taxis
In certain parts of Seoul – most pertinently the area around Myeongdong and City Hall – it can be extremely difficult to find a taxi willing to take you in the hours around midnight. At this time, minivans charging vastly inflated fees do the rounds, and they may be your only choice.

6 Traveling Uninsured
Traveling without adequate insurance is never wise, but it's a particularly bad idea in Seoul owing to the cost of health care. Also note that some policies do not cover travel in South Korea – so ensure that your policy is valid for the country before you travel.

7 Sticking to Seoul
The vast majority of travelers to South Korea never get further than Seoul. While the city certainly offers enough to see, to truly appreciate Korea, you'll have to head a little farther afield. There are many other lovely places to visit (see pp62–3), some of which can be visited on a half-day trip.

8 Trouble Areas
While South Korea is generally a safe country, there are certain areas where it pays to be a little more cautious. There is the occasional petty theft at Seoul's main train station as well as in the nightlife hot spots of Itaewon and Hongdae.

9 Buses
Few travelers end up making use of Seoul's bus system, largely because there is almost no signage in English at the stops, nor on the buses themselves. Add long numbers and a confusing color-coded system to the mix, and most visitors decide that it's usually best to take the subway or hop into a taxi.

10 Club Day
Hongdae's Club Day takes place once a month, and in theory it sounds great – W15,000 gets you free entry to 21 of the area's clubs, and one free drink. In practice, it can be hard to visit more than a few of the inevitably packed clubs in one night – even getting your hands on that free drink can become an ordeal.

Left **ATM machine** Center **Talking on a mobile phone** Right **Board displaying exchange rates**

🔟 Banking and Communications

1 Money
The national currency is the *won* (W), which comes in notes of W50,000, W10,000, W5,000, and W1,000, and coins of W500, W100, W50, and W10. The colors of the W5,000 and W50,000 are a little close for comfort; mercifully, few Koreans would ever dream of taking advantage of any resultant confusion.

2 Banks
Banks are usually open Monday to Friday, 9am to 4pm, and all are able to convert major international currencies into Korean *won*. Most banks will have at least one English-speaking member of staff – you are most likely to find one at KB or Shinhan banks, which have branches all over the city.

3 Changing Money
Incheon Airport's 24-hour booths are the best places to change money after arrival in Korea. At banks it may be tricky to track down an English-speaking member of staff, and when they're closed one has to resort to hotels, which generally offer poor rates.

4 ATMs
Most banks have international card-friendly ATMs, though connection can be hit and miss – you may have to try a few different banks before finding success. These are usually open round the clock, barring a couple of off-service hours very early in the morning.

5 Internet Access
Seoul probably has the world's greatest concentration of Internet cafés – just look for the "PC" signs. Such places are inevitably smoky affairs packed with locals taking part in online gaming sessions – no Koreans use Internet cafés to check their emails. Rates usually start at W1,500 per hour, with a 1-hour minimum. Finding Wi-Fi hotspots is usually simple too – Tom N Toms, Homestead, Holly's, and Ti-amo are among the major café chains that offer free access. Most higher-end hotels charge daily fees of around W20,000 for connection; at the other end of the scale, the rooms of many newer motels have Internet-ready computer terminals.

6 Post
There's one post office in each city district, and you will usually be able to find your nearest one by looking on the maps by subway station exits. Most post offices are open Monday to Friday 9am to 6pm, and 9am to 1pm on Saturday.

7 Credit Cards
Hotels, shops, cafés, and restaurants are increasingly accepting credit cards. In general, any place that accepts local cards will be able to accept foreign ones too.

8 Cell Phones
The concept of just buying SIM cards alone does not exist in Seoul, and unless you have a quad-band handset, it is unlikely that your cell phone will work in Korea. Make sure you check with your service provider before traveling.

9 Renting Cell Phones
Booths at Incheon International Airport rent out cell phones to travelers. If you are staying for any longer than a couple of weeks, it may be cheaper to buy a simple prepaid handset in Seoul. Although you can register it yourself at a telephone showroom, doing so with a Korean friend will make everything a lot easier.

10 Television
All hotels have a few international channels. Even at cheaper establishments a quick channel-surf will usually bring up an English-language movie or program on local cable TV – thankfully these are almost always subtitled rather than dubbed.

Left **A Korean police car** Center **Traffic in Seoul** Right **Reception at a hospital**

Streetsmart

TOP10 Security and Health

1 Emergency Numbers
Dial 112 for the police, or 119 for the ambulance or fire department. It is usually possible to have your call forwarded to someone who speaks English. However, since this can take time, it is best to have a local make the call.

2 Police
Though you will probably see quite a few police officers patrolling the Palace Quarter, few foreign travelers end up having anything to do with them. If you do run into trouble, it's best to call your embassy for advice.

3 Hospitals
Most of Seoul's hospitals have English-speaking doctors. You will also find hospitals with 24-hour English-language information lines, and dedicated international clinics. ✆ *Severance Hospital: 134 Shinchondong; Map B2; 2228 5800 • Seoul National University Hospital: 28 Yeongeondong; Map D2; 2072 2890, 2072 0505*

4 Pharmacies and Doctors
You will find pharmacies, known locally as *yakguk*, on almost every major road in Seoul. Some are open around the clock, and most pharmacies will have at least one English-speaking member of staff on duty. For anything behind the counter you will need to present a doctor's prescription. A quick Internet search will bring up the doctors' clinics closest to you. Most doctors can speak at least a little English. Visit fees start at just under W10,000.

5 Dentists
The international clinic at Seoul National University Hospital, near Hyehwa station, has English-speaking dentists. ✆ *Seoul National University Hospital: 28 Yeongeondong; Map D2; 2072 0753*

6 Crime
Crime rates in South Korea's capital are incredibly low for such a large city, which may come as a pleasant surprise to most visitors. Petty theft is nearly nonexistent, as are drug use and its associated social side-effects.

7 Traffic
Drivers regularly run red lights in Seoul – especially those handling buses, taxis, or motorbikes. The police rarely act against the offenders on such occasions, though attempts to curb drunken driving have been stepped up in recent years. Also keep in mind that Seoul's sidewalks often double as surrogate parts of the road – watch out for speeding motorbikes and people parking cars.

8 Women Travelers
Seoul presents no particular challenges for women. It is a very safe city, and female travelers will rarely encounter any special problems. Those who do not match the typical petite frame of Korean women may, however, find it hard to track down suitable sizes in clothing.

9 Smoking
Although Korean cigarettes are pretty cheap by international standards, and available at street stands all over Seoul, the authorities are slowly clamping down on smoking. Hotels generally have nonsmoking floors, while cafés and larger restaurants have dedicated smoking areas. At smaller restaurants, and almost all bars, there will be an ashtray on every table.

10 Food and Water
Seoul's tap water is safe to drink, though you will rarely need to bother with it. Water fountains can be found all over the city, sterilized water is given out for free at most restaurants, and bottled water is cheap. One particular brand, "DMZ," is sourced from the demilitarized zone between North and South Korea.

Left **Food market near Dongdaemun** Center **Eating with chopsticks** Right **Menus on display**

⑩ Dining and Drinking Tips

1 Go Local
Korean cuisine is highly distinctive, and in global terms it is right up there with the very best. A lack of familiarity scares some foreign travelers toward pizza, burgers, sandwiches, and the like, but it would be a shame to leave Korea without giving its food a try – chances are you'll love it.

2 Sharing
Koreans rarely dine alone, and most meals are made for sharing. This may seem alien to some visitors, but it certainly makes the dining experience a lot more fun, particularly with something like a barbecued meat feast. In group situations, just follow what the locals do. Although there are innumerable rules of etiquette to obey, foreigners are usually forgiven any slips in this regard.

3 Chopsticks
Most Korean meals are eaten with chopsticks, although foreigners might sometimes be provided with a fork instead. If you have never tried eating with chopsticks before, give it a go – most people pick it up fairly quickly, much to the surprise of the locals.

4 Vegetarians
Korea isn't exactly a vegetarian's paradise. Although vegetables feature prominently in almost all meals, few are vegetarian-only, and even those that are might have been prepared with the same utensils used for cooking meat.

5 Menus
While an admirable number of Seoul's restaurants have English-language menus, many at the cheaper end of the scale do not. It's worth noting that deciphering Korean menus is perhaps the fastest means of learning the Korean alphabet. With a little effort, it might not be as difficult as you expect.

6 Ordering
You'll be approached by restaurant staff as soon as you look ready to order. On occasions in which linguistic difficulties force you to point at menu items, try to point horizontally – some locals may interpret "I want the item under my finger" as "I want the item directly above my finger."

7 Paying
The highly Confucian nature of Korean society means that it is customary for hosts to pay, and locals almost never split the bill when eating with each other.

However, they may offer to perform this task when eating with foreigners. The sight of foreign travelers bickering over who should pay what will likely elicit laughter from restaurant staff.

8 Tipping
Tipping is another concept largely alien to Koreans – leave even a small bit of change in the hands of your waiter or waitress, and they'll probably chase you down the road with it.

9 Opening Hours
Koreans have the longest average working hours on the planet, and restaurants are no exception to the rule. Most places open up in the morning and close in the late evening, while some even stay open all night. It's certain that as long as you have cash, you won't ever go hungry.

10 Convenience Stores
Convenience stores such as 7-Eleven, CU, Buy the Way, and GS25 are on almost every street, and all are open 24 hours a day, every day of the year. All sell snacks, sandwiches, noodles, soft drinks, alcohol, and more, and in warmer months the tables and chairs set outside make a super-cheap alternative to bars.

Note: Please contact the restaurants for specific opening hours.

Left **Shoppers in Apgujeong, Central Seoul** Center **Cameras on sale** Right **Coex Mall**

Shopping Tips

1 Opening Hours
Most shops open at 9am or 10am, and stay open until late evening, with the exception of department stores, which close at around 6pm. Many travelers make nighttime visits to shops that have no opening hours at all – certain parts of Dongdaemun (see p82) and Namdaemun (see p78) markets are open around the clock.

2 VAT Refunds
Buy any product with a "Tax-Free Shopping" mark, and you'll be able to claim a VAT refund at the airport when leaving the country. However, the process is a little complicated, so if you plan on making use of the refunds, it's best to inquire about the details at the airport when you arrive in Seoul.

3 Malls and Department Stores
There are surprisingly few shopping malls in Seoul – IFC, Coex Mall, and Times Square (see p102), are the only true malls in the city. Department stores are a different matter, and you'll find them in every city district – the most notable being Shinsegae Department Store in Myeongdong (see p77) and Galleria in Apgujeong (see p102). ◈ IFC: 10 Gookjegeumyoongro • Map B4

4 Markets
There are lots of markets all over Seoul, and most are utterly fascinating. The most famous one is Dongdaemun, although Namdaemun, a slightly smaller competitor stretching north of Hoehyeon station, is also definitely worth a visit.

5 Designer Shops
Apgujeong, an area south of the river, is Seoul's prime designer-label territory. Flagship stores of the main international brands dot Apgujeongno, the area's main road, while boutiques selling top local brands can be found on the side-streets burrowing towards Dosan Park. ◈ Map F4

6 Textiles
Dongdaemun Market is the best place to head for fabric – some shop proprietors can speak enough English to make by-the-meter sales, and international credit cards are usually accepted. There are also lots of places selling hanbok, Korea's silky national costume.

7 Souvenirs
Insadong is by far the best place to head for goods such as pottery, tea sets, rice cakes, art supplies, and handmade paper (see pp12–13).

8 Electronics
Yongsan Electronics Market (see p57) and Techno Mart are Seoul's two main electronics malls, and both are absolutely huge. Techno Mart is a little farther away from the city center, though goods tend to be a bit cheaper. Although conning is relatively rare, it is certainly an issue, particularly at Yongsan Electronics Market. ◈ Techno Mart: 546–4 Gueidong • Map H4

9 Food
Those staying in Seoul for a while may soon be craving foreign foodstuffs. E-Mart, with branches around the city, is the best option, although Lotte Department Store (see p82) is more central. The Itaewon area also has a few smaller shops selling international ingredients.

10 Books
All of Seoul's large bookstores have foreign-language sections. Youngpoong and Kyobo have good selections. However, What the Book?, a large English-only store near the Itaewon station is by far the best. ◈ Youngpoong: 33 Seorindong; Map L4 • Kyobo: Life Building 1 Jongno 1-ga; Map L3 • What the Book?: 176–2 Itaewondong; Map R5; 797 2342

Left Outdoor pool at the Grand Hyatt **Center** Stylish room at the W Seoul Walkerhill

Luxury Hotels

1 Park Hyatt
Guests will feel quite special when checking in at the top-floor reception of this stunning hotel – and this is magnified when moving to the rooms. The designer rooms have compact, Zen-style furnishings.
◈ 995–14 Daechidong • Map F6 • 2016 1234 • www.seoul.park.hyatt.com • WWWWW

2 W Seoul Walkerhill
Aimed at 20- and 30- somethings, this is a favorite with honeymooning Koreans. The snazzy rooms feature Jacuzzis, while the common areas include super-trendy bars and cafés. ◈ 21 Gwangjangdong • Map D2 • 465 2222 • www.wseoul.com • WWWW

3 The Westin Chosun
South Korea's first top-end hotel is still one of its best. There are superb restaurants, and on-site facilities, and the helpful, well-trained staff are without equal in Seoul.
◈ 87–1 Sogongdong • Map L5 • 771 0500 • www.echosunhotel.com • WWWWW

4 The Shilla
The most traditionally Korean of Seoul's 5-star hotels, The Shilla is a real hit with overseas visitors. Both rooms and common areas are filled with charming accoutrements,

and there's a spa on site.
◈ 202 Jangchungdong • Map D3 • 2233 3131 • www.shilla.net • WWWWW

5 The Plaza
This top-quality hotel has a central location overlooking City Hall and Seoul Plaza, and boasts amenities such as a spa, fitness center, and an indoor swimming pool. Note that music events take place every summer evening in Seoul Plaza. ◈ 119 Sogongno • Map L5 • 771 2200 • www.hotelthe plaza.com • WWWW

6 JW Marriott
A classy hotel conveniently located atop a junction of three subway lines and Seoul's main bus terminal. There is a spa, fitness club, on-site restaurant, and indoor pool, and the upper floors offer excellent river views. ◈ 19–3 Banpodong • Map D5 • 6282 6262 • www.marriott.com • WWWWW

7 Grand Hyatt
Located partway up Namsan (see pp18–19), a mountain in the center of Seoul, this hotel offers a superb view of the city from most of its rooms and restaurants, all of which are top drawer. It also has an excellent on-site bar, JJ Mahoney's (see p88). ◈ 322 Sowollo • Map S5 • 797 1234 • www.seoul.grand.hyatt.com • WWWWW

8 Coex Intercontinental
Marginally the classier of the two Intercontinental hotels that top-and-tail the large Coex shopping mall. The north-end rooms look out over the charming Bongeunsa temple (see p97). ◈ 524 Bongeunsaro • Map F5 • 3452 2500 • www.seoul.intercontinental.com • WWWW

9 Sheraton D Cube
Part of the stunning, D Cube City complex, this 41-floor hotel is extremely well-designed. There is an indoor pool, and a virtual Screen Golf Course and Driving Range, on the 27th floor. There is also an on-site spa. The location is a little inconvenient for sightseeing, though ideal for those doing business in nearby Yeouido. ◈ 662 Gyeonginro • Map A4 • 2211 2000 • www.sheratonseouldcubecity.co.kr • WWWWW

10 Fraser Suites
The best of Seoul's smattering of serviced residences – most guests are here for weeks or months, but shorter stays are also possible. Service is excellent, rooms are huge, and there is a rooftop golf driving range and an on-site swimming pool.
◈ 272 Nakwondong • Map N4 • 6262 8888 • seoul.frasershospitality.com • WWWW

Most of Seoul's top-end hotels are served by direct shuttle buses from the airport – check www.airport.kr for information.

Price Categories

For a standard, double room per night (with breakfast if included), taxes and extra charges.

W under W60,000
WW W60,000–100,000
WWW W100,000–250,000
WWWW W250,000–400,000
WWWWW over W400,000

Left **Ibis hotel signage** Right **Reception, IP Boutique hotel**

TOP 10 Mid-Range Hotels

1 Metro Hotel
A splendid little mid-range hotel tucked into the Myeongdong shopping district. The rooms and service standards are far higher than you would expect at this price range, and there are hundreds of restaurants within a few minutes' walk. Breakfast is complimentary, and there's free Wi-Fi as well. ◈ 199–33 Euljiro 2-ga • Map M5 • 752 1112 • www.metrohotel.co.kr • WWW

2 Ibis Myeongdong
Excellent customer service, great buffet breakfasts, and a highly accessible location more than compensate for the slightly small rooms at Ibis Myengdong. There's a gym and a restaurant on site. ◈ 59–5 Myeongdong 1-ga • Map M6 • 6361 8888 • www.ibishotel.com • WWWWW

3 Doulos Hotel
This simple hotel is located in downtown Seoul. The guest rooms on offer are basic yet comfortable, and impeccably clean. ◈ 111 Gwansudong • Map N4 • 2266 2244 • www.douloshotel.com • WWW

4 IP Boutique
This hotel has more than 100 rooms, all designed with care. There is a restaurant on site, and Itaewon's cosmopolitan array of restaurants is only a short walk away. ◈ 737–32 Hannamdong • Map S5 • 3702 8000 • www.ipboutiquehotel.com • WWWW

5 Gangnam Artnouveau City II
Huge, richly decorated rooms are set in a serviced residence located on a fascinating Gangnam side-street. Substantial discounts on the rack rates are usually available, particularly for longer-term stays. There's a fitness center on site, an Italian restaurant, and a garden located on top of the building. ◈ 1330–4 Seochodong • Map D6 • 580 7500 • www.artnouveaucity.co.kr • WWWWW

6 Prince Hotel
Smart hotel with a great location – across the road from the busy Myeongdong shopping district, though without the bustle. There is a range of color-coordinated rooms to choose from, and a coffee shop with a lounge. ◈ 1–1 Namsandong 2-ga • Map D3 • 752 7111 • www.hotelprinceseoul.co.kr • WWW

7 Royal Hotel
At the upper end of mid-range, the Royal Hotel offers beautifully decorated rooms, and a plethora of shopping and dining opportunities right on its doorstep. The hotel also has a spa, bar, and restaurant. ◈ 6 Myeongdong 1-ga • Map D2 • 756 1112 • www.royal.co.kr • WWWWW

8 Yoido
This is an affordable option in the Yeouido business district. The rooms and common areas are good value for the price, there is a 24-hour fitness center, and the delightful Hangang riverside is just a stone's throw away. ◈ 10–3 Yeouidodong • Map A4 • 782 0121 • www.yoidohotel.co.kr • WWW

9 Best Western Premier Kukdo
Smart, tourist-friendly hotel overlooking Euljiro, and within easy walking distance of Myeongdong, Cheonggyecheon, and Insadong. Some upper-floor rooms have views of Namsan. ◈ 310 Euljiro 4-ga • Map M5 • 6466 1234 • www.hotelkukdo.com • WWW

10 PJ Hotel
Hugely popular with Japanese tourists, meaning that excellent customer service and sky-high standards of cleanliness are almost a given. There are two restaurants and a café in the hotel. Wi-Fi access is free for guests, and the hotel also offers a women-only floor. ◈ 73–1 Inhyeondong • Map P5 • 2280 7013 • www.hotelpj.co.kr • WWWWW

← Unless stated otherwise, all hotels accept credit cards, and have private bathrooms and air conditioning.

115

Left **Bukchon Guesthouse** Center **Courtyard, Sophia Guesthouse** Right **Anguk Guesthouse**

Traditional Hanok

1 Bukchon Guesthouse

A collection of three small guesthouses which together provide a wide range of rooms – some small, some fairly large. ◎ 72 Gyedong • Map M2 • 6711 6717 • www.bukchon72.com • WW

2 Bongsan Guesthouse

This appealing guesthouse has simple rooms arrayed around a small courtyard. It is located just off a delightful residential street, which, though old-fashioned in nature, is home to an increasing number of trendy cafés and restaurants. ◎ 73–6 Gyedong • Map M2 • 745 6638 • www.bongsan house.com • WW

3 Seoul Guesthouse

Perhaps the most laidback option among the Bukchon hanok guesthouses, this is only five minutes away from central Seoul. There are a wide number of rooms to choose from – some surprisingly modern, given the secluded location. ◎ 135–1 Gyedong • Map M2 • 745 0057 • www.seoul110.com • WW

4 Woorijib Hanok Guesthouse

This guesthouse has three simple rooms, each featuring a little bar, bedding, and wooden

chests. In the common areas you'll find guitars to strum, as well as free coffee, tea, and toast in the kitchen. Note that the name, meaning "our house," is spelled in a confusing variety of ways. ◎ 104–3 Gyedong • Map M2 • 744 0536 • www.wooriguest.com • WWW

5 Yoo's Family Guesthouse

The owners make great efforts to please international guests, making this the friendliest hanok option in the area. They have two locations in a wonderful area, just to the west of the Jongmyo shrine (see p68). ◎ 156 Gwonnongdong • Map N2 • 3673 3266 • www. yoosfamily.com • W

6 Anguk Guesthouse

Upon request, the gracious owners will pick you up from the Anguk subway station, as the guesthouse is hard to track. Guests are offered a range of delicious teas and, unlike in some other hanok options, there are Western-style beds in the rooms. ◎ 72–3 Angukdong • Map M2 • 736 8304 • www.anguk-house.com • WW

7 Sophia Guesthouse

Dating from the 1860s, this is the oldest hanok guesthouse in the area. The rooms are suitably

traditional in feel and the decor is superb. ◎ 157–1 Sogyeokdong • Map L2 • 720 5467 • WWW

8 Rakkojae

This higher-end option has beautifully manicured gardens and gorgeous period furniture, and serves traditional meals and tea – all in a genuine 1870s hanok. However, the owners are not always accommodating, and the rooms are rather overpriced. ◎ 98 Gyedong • Map M2 • 742 3410 • www.rkj.co.kr • WWWWW

9 Tea Guesthouse

Rooms here are modern according to hanok standards, and have TVs and computers with Internet access. The common areas, however, are traditional, with gorgeous folding screens, period furniture, and decorative walls. Small tea ceremonies are also held here. ◎ 131–1 Gyedong • Map M2 • 3675 9877 • www. teaguesthouse.com • WW

10 Hanok Homestay

A wonderful program giving visitors the chance to stay with residents of the neighborhood. Properties vary in quality, but owners are almost uniformly friendly with a real desire to introduce Korean culture to visitors. ◎ 2148 1855 • homestay. jongno.go.kr • W

Price Categories

For a standard, double room per night (with breakfast if included), taxes and extra charges.

W	under W60,000
WW	W60,000–100,000
WWW	W100,000–250,000
WWWW	W250,000–400,000
WWWWW	over W400,000

Jogyesa temple, part of the Templestay program

TOP 10 Budget Stays

1 J-Hill
A relative newbie in the Myeongdong area, J-Hill is a great choice. The rooms may be small but the staff are amiable and helpful, and the breakfasts fantastic. There's also a wonderful viewing balcony – a brilliant place to have a cup of coffee. ◎ 33–1 Myeongdong • Map M6 • 753 8900 • www.jhill.kr • WWW

2 Sunbee
Though a little old-fashioned for some, Sunbee is easy on the budget. Rooms contain everything you'll need, as well as some extras such as hairdryers, toiletries, and cable TV. ◎ 198–11 Gwanhundong • Map M3 • 730 3451 • WW

3 Come Inn Guesthouse
The best of the Hongdae area's many hostels, Come Inn is not only nearer to the bars, but offers facilities that would also put some hotels to shame. Guests can make use of laptops, play CDs, and hang out on the balcony with fellow travelers. ◎ 358–91 Seogyodong • Map A3 • 9493 7279 • www.comeinnkorea.com • W

4 Jelly Hotel
While most of Seoul's love motels hide behind a wafer-thin veneer of respectability, this one is proud of its purpose – ironically, this has made it popular with travelers as well. Each room has been jazzed up with a jacuzzi, mirror-tiling and the like, while some have heart-shaped beds. ◎ 648–7 Yeoksamdong • Map F5 • 553 4737 • WWW

5 Hotel D'Oro
A cheap Itaewon hotel situated off the main street – far enough to eliminate almost all of the noise. The rooms here are fine for the price, and surprisingly clean for the area – at this price level, you seriously needn't look elsewhere. ◎ 124–3 Itaewondong • Map R5 • 749 6525 • WW

6 Hotel Biz
Biz is a simple affair tucked into the old-fashioned, but highly atmospheric, side-streets off Euljiro. Though nominally a hotel, it has more the feel of a youth hostel – albeit one with clean, private rooms. ◎ 335–2 Euljiro 3-ga • Map M5 • 2266 1553 • hotelbizseoul.priorguest.com • WW

7 Hotel M
A business hotel, M has large, clean rooms designed along five different color schemes. All the en suite bathrooms boast excellent power showers, and some have small whirlpool bathtubs. There's also a chic café-bar on site. ◎ 14–23 Yeouidodong • Map A4 • 783 2271 • www.hotelm.co.kr • WWW

8 Tria
A south-of-the-river hotel, with rooms that are astonishingly well designed for the price. Suites don't cost much more than the regular rooms. There's also a funky on-site bar. ◎ 677–11 Yeoksamdong • Map F5 • 553 2471 • www.triahotel.co.kr • WWW

9 Innostel
This government-sponsored program brings together Seoul's more visitor-friendly budget stays. There is a wide range of locations and price categories. ◎ innostel.visitseoul.net • W

10 Templestay
A unique cultural program, Templestay enables foreign visitors to spend the night at temples across South Korea and experience the life of Buddhist practitioners. Bongeunsa (see p97) and Jogyesa (see p10) are among the temples in Seoul that are a part of this program. The temples serve only vegetarian food, and guests have to wake up early to take part in temple routines. ◎ eng.templestay.com • W

General Index

Acknowledgments

The Author

Martin Zatko is a travel writer and consultant specializing in East Asia. He has written almost 20 travel guides, including half a dozen about the Korean peninsula. He first visited Seoul in 2002, just before the World Cup came to town, and the city has been a home from home for him ever since.

Photographer James Tye

Additional Photography
Tim Draper

Fact Checker Won Jang

At DK INDIA

Managing Editor
MadhuMadhavi Singh

Editorial Manager
Sheeba Bhatnagar

Design Manager Mathew Kurien

Project Editor Divya Chowfin

Editor Gayatri Mishra

Project Designer Vinita Venugopal

Assistant Cartographic Manager
Suresh Kumar

Cartographer Sachin Pradhan

Picture Research Manager
Taiyaba Khatoon

Picture Researcher Nikhil Verma

Senior DTP Designer
Azeem Siddiqui

Indexer Helen Peters

Proofreader Aruna Ghose

At DK LONDON

Publisher Vivien Antwi

List Manager Christine Stroyan

Senior Editor Sadie Smith

Editor Vicki Allen

Designer Tracy Smith

Senior Cartographic Manager
Casper Morris

Senior DTP Designer Jason Little

Production Controller
Charlotte Cade

Special Assistance Jiyun Jeong

Photography Permissions

Dorling Kindersley would like to thank the following for their assistance and kind permission to photograph at their establishments:

Arario Gallery; Asian Art Museum; Hansangsoo Embroidery Museum; Gana Art Gallery; Gwacheon National Science Museum; Kukje Gallery; Leeum, Samsung Museum of Art; National Museum of Korea; National Museum of Contemporary Art; Owl Art & Craft Museum; Seoul Museum of Art; Seoul Museum of History; Seodaemun Prison History Hall; Seoul Sun Gallery and Art Centre; Whanki Art Gallery; World Jewellery Museum.

Picture Credits

Placement Key: a-above; b-below/bottom; c-centre; f-far; l-left; r-right; t-top

Works of art have been reproduced with the kind permission of the following copyright holders:

Recycling Haechi © Choi Jeong-Hwa 17t; *Walking Woman* © Jonathan Borofsky 28tc; *The Triumph of Daily Life* © Hannah Kim 28tr.

The publisher would like to thank the following for their kind permission to reproduce their photographs:

ALAMY IMAGES: David Ball 64–65; Derek Brown 25c; dbtravel 40tr; INTERFOTO 35tl; JTB Photo 48–49; Kruppa 36tr; MarioPonta 91bl; mediacolor's 1; PictureLake 32–33; Prisma Archivo 97br; SFL Travel 104–105.

BAMBOO HOUSE: 100tr.

BRICX: 94tr.

CORBIS: Pascal Deloche 93cl; Owen Franken 34tr; Park Jin Hee 36tl; Krause Johansen 34tl.

CRAFTWORKS TAPHOUSE: 54tc, 38tl.

DREAMSTIME.COM: Anizza 16–17c; Sebastian Czapnik 98tr; Michael Kirkham 63t; Ragsac19 37cl; Yejun 19bl.

FOTOLIA: ItinerantLens 36bl; Skelectron 62bl.

GETTY IMAGES: Alec Haskard 80–81; Martin Moos 23cr, 87cl.

GRAND HYATT SEOUL: 88tr, 114tl.

JASENG HOSPITAL OF KOREAN EASTERN MEDICINE: 58tr.

O KITCHEN: 89tc.

PLATOON KUNSTHALLE: 54cr.

SANGSANGMADANG: 90tr.

SUPERSTOCK: Marka 34cr.

T-LOUND: 54tr, 103tr.

THE SHILLA SEOUL: 58cr.

W SEOUL WALKERHILL: 114tr.

All other images are © Dorling Kindersley.

For further information see: www.dkimages.com.

Special Editions of DK Travel Guides

DK Travel Guides can be purchased in bulk quantities at discounted prices for use in promotions or as premiums. We are also able to offer special editions and personalized jackets, corporate imprints, and excerpts from all of our books, tailored specifically to meet your own needs.

To find out more, please contact:
(in the United States) **SpecialSales@dk.com**
(in the UK) **travelspecialsales@uk.dk.com**
(in Canada) DK Special Sales at **general@tourmaline.ca**
(in Australia) **business.development@pearson.com.au**

Phrase Book

The Korean language uses an alphabet called the Hangeul. Pronouncing Korean words is a tough task – some sounds simply do not have English-language equivalents. For example, there's only one character for "l" and "r", with the sound somewhere in between the two. The letters "k," "d," "b," and "j" are often written "k," "t," "p," and "ch," and are pronounced approximately halfway towards those Roman equivalents. Consonants are fairly easy to master – note that some are doubled up, and spoken more forcefully. See the Guidelienes for Pronunciation for some of the tricky vowels and dipthongs (British English readings offer the closest equivalents).

Guidelines for Pronunciation: Consonants

Note that some consonants are pronounced differently depending upon whether they start or finish a syllable. In these cases, the terminal readings have been given in parentheses.

ㄱ	g (k)		ㅗ	o
ㄴ	n		ㅛ	yo
ㄷ	d (t)		ㅜ	u
ㄹ	r/l		ㅠ	yu
ㅁ	m		ㅡ	eu
ㅂ	b (p)		ㅣ	i
ㅅ	s (t)		ㅔ	e
ㅈ	j (t)		ㅐ	ae
ㅊ	ch (t)		ㅖ	ye
ㅋ	k		ㅒ	yae
ㅌ	t		ㅟ	wi
ㅍ	p		ㅞ	we
ㅎ	h		ㅙ	wae
ㅇ	ng		ㅘ	wa
ㅏ	a		ㅚ	oe
ㅑ	ya		ㅢ	ui
ㅓ	eo		ㅝ	wo
ㅕ	yeo			

Vowels

a	as in "car"
ya	as in "yap"
eo	as in "hot"
yeo	as in "yob"
o	pronounced "ore"
yo	pronounced as "your"
u	as in "Jew"
yu	pronounced "you"
eu	no English equivalent; widen your mouth and try an "euggh"sound of disgust
i	as in "pea"

Useful Phrases

Yes	ye/ne	예/네
No	aniyo	아니요
Please (asking for something)	…juseyo	…주세요
Excuse me	shillye hamnida	실례합니다
I'm sorry	mian hamnida	미안합니다
Thank you	gamsa hamnida	감사합니다

Do you speak English?	yeongeo halsu-isseoyo?	영어 할 수 있어요?
Is there someone who can speak English?	yeongeo-reul haljul a-neun bun isseoyo?	영어를 할 줄 아는 분 있어요?
I can't speak Korean	jeo-neun hangugeo-reul mot haeyo	저는 한국어를 못 해요
Please help me	dowa-juseyo	도와 주세요
Hello; Good morning/ afternoon/ evening	annyeong haseyo	안녕 하세요
Hello (polite)	annyeong hashimnikka	안녕 하십니까
How are you?	jal jinaesseoyo?	잘 지냈어요?
I'm fine	jal jinaesseoyo /jo-ayo	잘 지냈어요 / 좋아요

Directions and Places

Where is (x)?	-i/ga eodi-eyo?	-이/가 어디에 요?
Straight ahead	jikjin	직진
Left	oen-jjok (pronounced "wen-chok")	왼쪽
Right	oreun-jjok	오른쪽
Behind	dwi-ae	뒤에
In front of	ap-ae	앞에
Map	maep/jido	맵/지도
Entrance	ip-gu	입구
Exit	chul-gu	출구
Museum	bangmulgwan	박물관
Park	gongwon	공원
Temple	Jeol/sachal	절/사찰
Toilet	hwajang-shil	화장실
Tourist office	gwan-gwang annaeso	관광 안내소

Staying in a Hotel

Hotel	hotel	호텔
Motel	motel	모텔
Guesthouse	yeogwan	여관
Budget guesthouse	yeoinsuk	여인숙
Rented room	minbak	민박
Youth hostel	yuseu hoseutel	유스 호스텔
Korean-style room	ondol-bang	온돌방
Western-style room	chimdae-bang	침대방
Single room	shinggeul chimdae	싱글 침대
Double room	deobeul chimdae	더블 침대
Twin room	chimdae dugae	침대 두 개
En-suite room	yokshil-ddallin bang	욕실 달린방
Shower	syaweo	샤워
Bath	yokjo	욕조
Key	ki	키
Passport	yeogwon	여권
Do you have any vacancies?	bang isseoyo?	방 있 어요?
How much is the room?	bang-i eolma -eyo?	방이 얼마에요?
Does that include breakfast?	gagyeok-e achim-shiksa poham-dwae isseoyo?	가격에 아침식사 포함돼 있어요?
I have a reservation	jeo-neun yeyak haesseoyo	저는 예약 했어요

I don't have a reservation	jeo-neun yeyak anhaesseoyo	저는 예약 안했어요
One/two/three nights	haru/ iteol/ samil + bam	하룻밤/이틀밤/삼일밤
One week	il-ju-il	일주일
May I see the room?	bang bol-su isseoyo?	방 좀 수 있어요?

Health

Hospital	byeongwon	병원
Pharmacy	yak-guk	약국
Medicine	yak	약
Doctor	uisa	의사
Dentist	chigwa-uisa	치과의사
Diarrhea	seolsa	설사
Nausea	meseukkeo-um	메스꺼움
Fever	yeol	열
Food poisoning	shikjungdok	식중독
Antibiotics	hangsaengje	항생제
Antiseptic	sodok-yak	독약
Penicillin	penishillin	페니실린
I'm ill	jeo-neun apayo	저는 아파요
I'm allergic to...	...allereugi-ga isseoyo	...알레르기가 있어요
It hurts here	yeogi-ga apayo	여기가 아파요
Please call a doctor	uisa-reul bulleo juseyo	의사를 불러 주세요

Keeping in Touch

Post office	uche-guk	우체국
Envelope	bongtu	봉투
Letter	pyeonji	편지
Postcard	yeopseo	엽서
Stamp	u-pyo	우표
Airmail	hanggong u-pyeon	항공 우편
Telephone	jeon-hwa	전화
Fax	paekseu	팩스
Telephone card	jeonhwa kadeu	전화카드
Internet café	PC-bang	PC 방
I would like to call...	...hante jeonhwa hago-shipeoyo	한테 전화하고 싶어요
May I speak to...	...jom baggwo juseyo	좀 바꿔 주세요

Eating Out

Waiter/Waitress (lit. "Here!")	yeogiyo!	여기요!
How much is that?	eolma-eyo?	얼마에요?
I would like...	...hago shipeoyo	...하고 싶어요
May I have the bill?	gyesanseo juseyo?	계산해 주세요
I'm a vegetarian	jeo-neun chaeshikju uija-eyo	저는 채식주의자에요
Chopsticks	jeot-garak	젓가락
Fork	po-keu	포크
Knife	nai-peu/kal	나이프/칼
Spoon	sut-garak	숟가락
Menu	menyu	메뉴
Delicious!	mashisseoyo!	맛있어요!

Menu Decoder

Black tea (lit. "red tea")	hong-cha	홍차
Green tea	nok-cha	녹차
Coffee	keopi	커피
Orange juice	orenji jyuseu	오렌지 쥬스
Fruit juice	gwa-il jyuseu	과일 쥬스
Milk	uyu	우유
Mineral water	saengsu	생수
Water	mul	물
Baekseju	baekseju	백세주
Beer	maekju	맥주
Bottled beer	byeong maekju	병 맥주
Draft beer	ssaeng maekju	생맥주
Makgeolli	makkeolli	막걸리
Wine	wain	와인
Whisky	wiseuki	위스키
Beef	so-gogi	쇠고기
Bibimbap	bibimbap	비빔밥
Bread	bbang	빵
Cheese	chi-jeu	치즈
Chicken	dak-gogi	닭고기
Duck meat	oti-gogi	오리고기
Dumplings	mandu	만두
Eggs	gyeran	계란
Fruit	gwa-il	과일
Fish	saengsun/ hoe (raw fish)	생선/회
Fried rice	bokkeumbap	볶음밥
Ham	haem	햄
kimchi	kimchi	김치
Noodles	myeon	면
Pork	dwaeji-gogi	돼지고기
Red-pepper paste	gochu-jang	고추장
Rice	bap	밥
Rice rolls	gimbap	김밥
Shrimp	sae-u	새우
Squid	ojing-eo	오징어
Tuna	chamchi	참치

Numbers

The Korean language uses two number systems: a native Korean system and a Sino-Korean system of Chinese origin.

The native Korean system only goes up to 99 and has been placed on the right-hand side of the readings.

0	yeong/gong	영/공
1	il/hana	일/하나
2	i (pronounced "ee")/dul	이/둘
3	sam/set	삼/셋
4	sa/net	사/넷
5	o/daseot	오/다섯
6	yuk/yeoseot	육/여섯
7	chil/ilgop	칠/일곱
8	pal/yeodeol	팔/여덟
9	gu/ahop	구/아홉
10	ship/yeol	십/열
11	shib-il/ yeol-hana	십일/열하나
12	shib-I/yeol-dul	십이/열 둘
20	i-shib/seumul	이십/스물
30	sam-shib/ seoreun	삼십/서른
100	baek	백
200	i-baek	이백
1,000	cheon	천
10,000	man	만
100,000	sim-man	십만
1,000,000	baeng-man	백만
100,000,000	eok	억

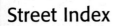

Street Index